Native Plants of British Columbia's Coastal Dry Belt

NATIVE PLANTS OF BRITISH COLUMBIA'S COASTAL DRY BELT

A Photographic Guide

Hans Roemer & Mary Sanseverino

HARBOUR PUBLISHING

1 2 3 4 5 — 29 28 27 26 25

Harbour Publishing Co. Ltd.
P.O. Box 219, Madeira Park, BC, V0N 2H0
www.harbourpublishing.com

Edited by Noel Hudson
Cover design by Anna Comfort O'Keeffe
Text design by Libris Simas Ferraz / Onça Publishing
Printed and bound in South Korea

Harbour Publishing acknowledges the support of the Canada Council for the Arts, the Government of Canada, and the Province of British Columbia through the BC Arts Council.

Library and Archives Canada Cataloguing in Publication

Title: Native plants of British Columbia's coastal dry belt : a photographic guide / Hans Roemer & Mary Sanseverino.
Names: Roemer, Hans (Ecologist), author | Sanseverino, Mary, 1957- author.
Description: Includes bibliographical references and index.
Identifiers: Canadiana (print) 20240527801 | Canadiana (ebook) 20240527828 | ISBN 9781998526000 (softcover) | ISBN 9781998526017 (EPUB)
Subjects: LCSH: Endemic plants—British Columbia—Pacific Coast—Pictorial works. | LCSH: Endemic plants—British Columbia—Pacific Coast—Identification.
Classification: LCC QK203.B7 R64 2025 | DDC 580.9711/1—dc23

Contents

Tables and Figures

Acknowledgements

WE WOULD LIKE TO THANK OUR REVIEWERS, ANDY MacKINNON, JIM POJAR, Nancy Turner and Bob Turner, who took the time to look at various successive versions of our manuscript: Andy MacKinnon, for making important connections for us and for his overall suggestions and frequent encouragement; Jim Pojar, for a very thorough review in writing; Nancy Turner, for comments and discussions that both enlightened and intrigued us; and Bob Turner, for assessing and commenting on overall readability and presentation. All of you were beyond generous with your knowledge, time and expertise, and this guide is much the better for it.

Our gratitude is also due to Del Meidinger, who produced the map of the Coastal Douglas-fir Moist Maritime Biogeoclimatic Zone.

Ryan Batten's review and updating of botanical names were greatly appreciated, and so was Terry McIntosh's inspection and correct naming of several bryophyte photographs.

Our long-suffering partners, Michael Whitney and Heidi Roemer, also contributed valuable general comments, and we thank them for this.

While everyone's work was very much appreciated, any errors, omissions or flaws lie entirely at the doorstep of the authors.

Hans Roemer would also like to emphasize that without early mentors, such as professors Reinhold Tüxen, Marc Bell and Nurettin Keser, and later colleagues in the field, including Adolf and Oluna Ceska, Trevor Goward, Curtis Bjork, Matt Fairbarns, Mike Miller, Jenifer Penny, Ryan Batten and numerous others, many more gaps would have remained in his botanical knowledge.

Mary Sanseverino would like to thank colleagues, students and friends from the University of Victoria's Department of Computer Science, the School of Environmental Studies and beyond for encouraging her work at the intersection of photography, the natural world and computer science. Particular thanks to Kristen Walsh, Mike Whitney, Jenna Falk, Alan MacLeod, Daniel German, Eric Higgs and Brian Starzomski: your insights continue to be guiding lights.

Many thanks from both of us to all of you!

Preface

THIS BOOK IS ALL ABOUT HELPING YOU, THE READER, BECOME MORE FAMILIAR with those plants that count toward conservation. In a much-modified landscape such as the coastal dry belt, native plants are the key to recognizing, evaluating and appreciating those precious remnants of what is left of once functioning ecosystems.

In 1967, when Hans Roemer arrived on Vancouver Island, many of the introduced plants were familiar to him, but the native plants were all new and fascinating to him—and fascinating they have remained to this day.

After an initial assistantship at the University of Victoria, he conducted field research to formally describe the forest ecosystems of the Saanich Peninsula. This included detailed records of the frequency and abundance of species making up the plant communities of the peninsula. His research culminated in a doctoral dissertation in 1972. Little did Hans know that these details would become crucial to the guide you now hold in your hands.

Hans went on to spend 18 years as a plant ecologist for the BC Ecological Reserves Program. He followed this with many years as a consultant, mainly in rare plant inventories, all of which further contributed to the information contained in this book.

Hans's research method, presenting plant diversity in definable communities and typical habitats, one at a time, is a defining feature of this guide. This approach has two main advantages: firstly, readers who use this technique deal with only those few species at a time that are typical for a particular community or habitat; secondly, the users of this guide get to know where to look for which species by using plant communities and habitats. Looking at plants in the context of communities and habitats leads us to think about the landscape in the way a plant ecologist might.

Conserving what is left of the original ecosystems is of the utmost importance today, despite the popular perception that disturbed ecosystems can be "restored." Once invaded by foreign plants, many ecosystems cannot be restored. We must therefore prioritize areas for protection according to the proportion of native versus introduced plants.

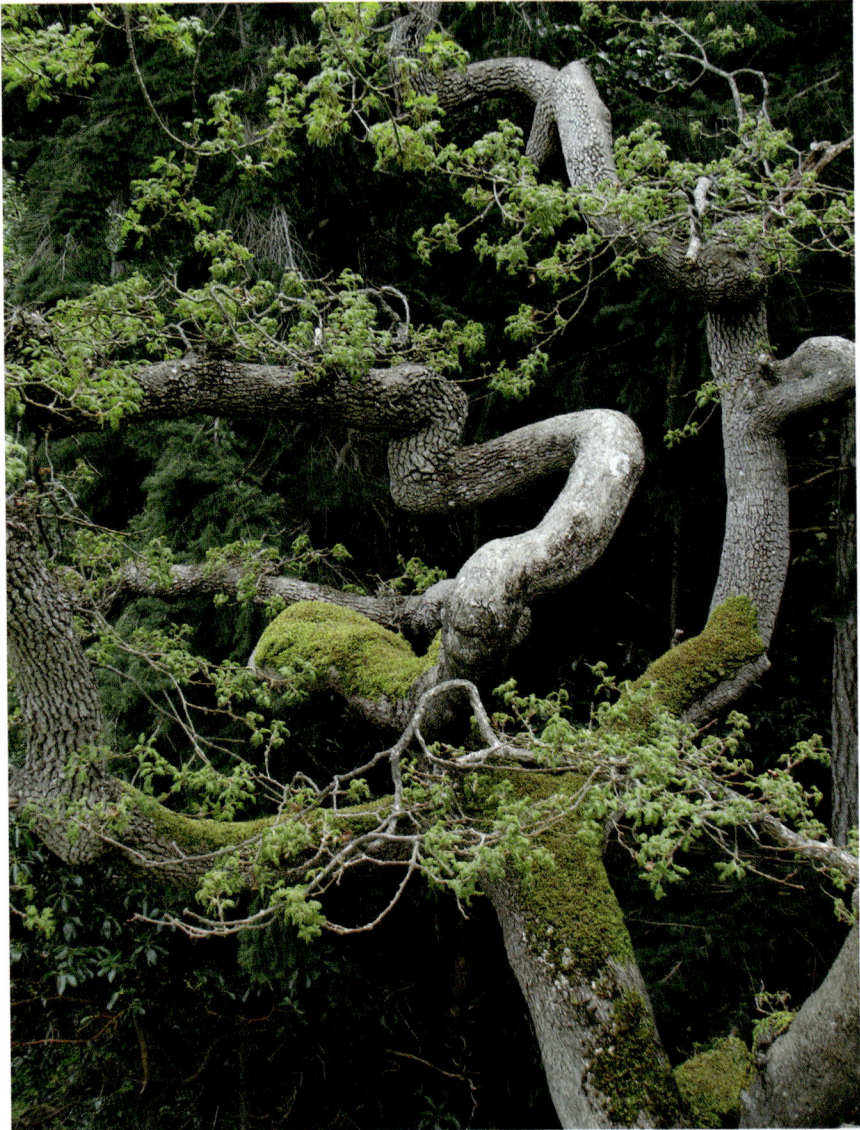

Quercus garryana (Garry oak).

Mary Sanseverino's strengths complement those of her co-author. As a former computer science faculty member at the University of Victoria, she knows how to handle text and images efficiently, as well as the appropriate software required for different parts of the project. Mary is also an accomplished photographer and shares Hans's enthusiasm for native plants.

Through a happy coincidence of mutual friends and acquaintances, we were able to bring our ecological, botanical, photographic and technical skills together in the production of this guide. It is almost something of a bonus that we both relish time spent in the natural environment. Any and all opportunities for field trips into the coastal dry belt were seized with gusto!

The result is a guidebook that enables you to not only identify and get to know over 500 of the most important plants of this special area, but also to learn in which community or habitat they are found. This is possible through the use of the photographs, descriptions in the text, and the included plant frequency lists, without the need for botanical plant identification keys. Details too minute to recognize at the scale of this volume may easily be zoomed in on if you also have the ebook version.

On a more emotional level, the motivation for this book was our desire to share and build knowledge: the more we know about an ecosystem, community or habitat, the more we tend to appreciate and nurture it. If this guide serves to make another biodiversity defender out of you, then we have met another important objective.

Regardless of what brings you to this guide, we hope you will enjoy using it as much as we enjoyed researching, writing and producing it. We wish you many happy trails through landscapes of wonder in BC's coastal dry belt.

Hans Roemer & Mary Sanseverino

About This Guide

How does this guide differ from other plant books?

Books on plants generally focus on the identification of species. They range from highly technical works relying on taxonomic keys to more popular approaches based on flower colour, and from volumes illustrated by austere black-and-white drawings to those featuring full-colour photographs. What they have in common is that they typically present large numbers of plant species from broad geographical areas, irrespective of their native environments.

This guide takes a different approach. It presents plant species in the context of their plant communities and habitats, one community or habitat type at a time. This is made possible by the fact that the species content of plant communities and well-circumscribed habitats is highly predictable.

This approach has several advantages. It allows us to deal with a small number of species at any one time (for instance, only 15 to 25 for a local forest community) and tells us what species to expect in a given environmental setting. With just a few species to concentrate on at a time, it is easy to identify them using the accompanying photographs.

Each of the first 10 section headings, named for a plant community or habitat, contains an image illustrating the community or habitat and a table listing its species combination. This is followed by photographs and brief comments on the individual species.

Who is this guide for?

This guide is designed with the average naturalist in mind. Great care was taken to avoid technical jargon. Some botanical terms proved impossible to replace; these are explained in a glossary at the back of the book. It is

hoped that this guide will also be suitable for novices who want to find out more about native plants and their environments, as well as for college- and university-level students, and for members of those many dedicated volunteer groups who are active in parks and protected areas.

Why focus on native species?

First off, we hope that knowledge gained from this guide will eventually result in increased conservation consciousness. In this context, native plants should carry a higher priority than introduced plants. Further, non-native species often blur the boundaries of native plant communities, rendering the present approach by community types less workable. Including all non-native species encountered in our area of interest would have greatly expanded the scope of this project and resulted in a less focused guide. However, the appendix, "Foreign Species Invasions," shows some of the introduced species that may become invasive in the plant communities and habitats featured in this book.

What and where is the coastal dry belt?

The mountains on Vancouver Island and the Olympic Mountains in adjacent Washington state create a "rain shadow" or "dry belt" covering the area outlined in yellow on the following map. The dry belt boundaries shown are those of the Coastal Douglas-fir Moist Maritime Biogeoclimatic Zone, as presented by the BC Forest Service (Nuszdorfer et al., 1991). This zone occurs in the area of mean annual precipitation between 650 and 1,250 millimetres and comprises the area of southeast Vancouver Island south of Comox, the Gulf Islands, and minor parts of the mainland coast. Also included are southern aspects of hills and small mountains to about 400 metres in elevation that bear strong dry belt features and contain native grasslands.

Tables and lists in this guide

At the beginning of each of the first 10 sections, readers will find a table listing the plant species that may be encountered in the respective plant community or habitat. It is important to realize that these tables or lists represent the "average" species combinations determined from surveying many different samples of the plant community or habitat. They also outline which plants will be covered in the section and show how likely (in percentage) a species is to be found in a given community or habitat.

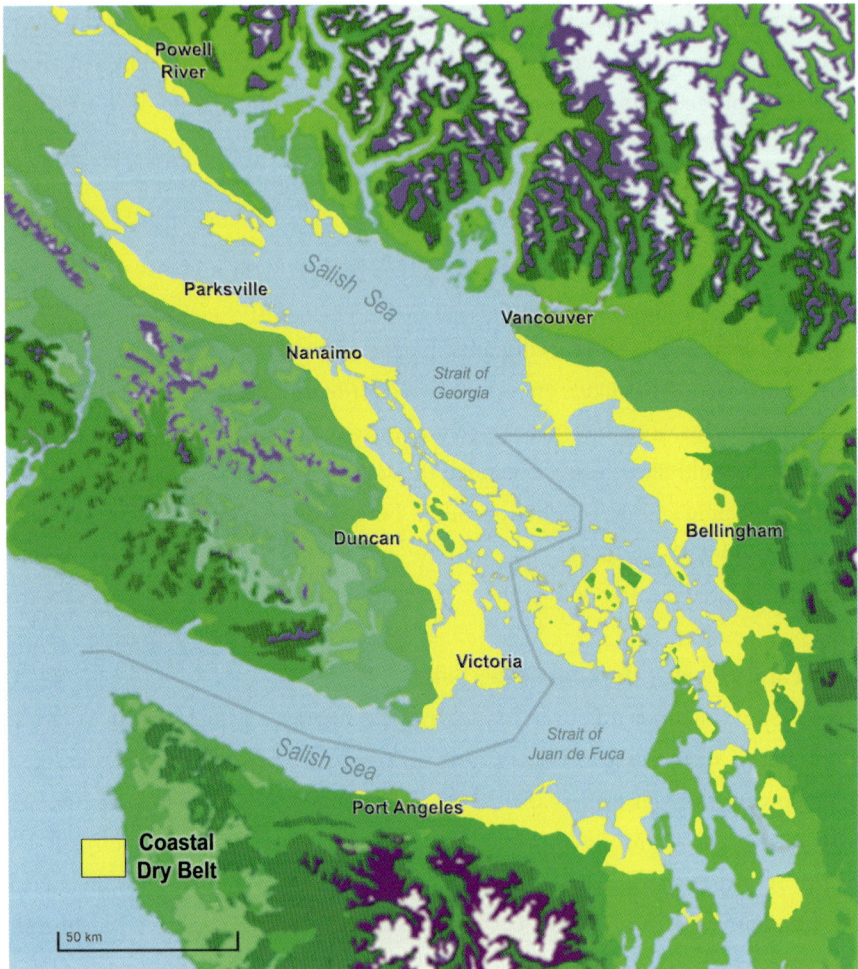

Figure 1: The coastal dry belt of British Columbia and adjacent areas of Washington state as portrayed by the Coastal Douglas-fir Moist Maritime Biogeoclimatic Zone. *Map produced by Del Meidinger, Meidinger Ecological Consultants Ltd., Victoria, BC, using publicly available biogeoclimatic map data and base map (© OpenStreetMap contributors: openstreetmap.org).*

Generation of plant community species lists

Over many years, Hans sampled local plant communities for the purpose of forest classification. This allowed him to calculate the percentage of species frequency for tables 1 to 10 of this guide. The following sample table is provided to demonstrate how the percentages are determined. Note that the actual species names are replaced by numbers to demonstrate the calculation method rather than the floristic description (original data available from the authors upon request).

Sample Table: Pacific wormwood and fescue plant community

% species frequency in plant community

("x" denotes presence of species)
1–16: Sample lists representing this plant community

Plant name	%	1	2	3	4	5	6	7	8	9	10	11	12	13	14	15	16
Species 1	100	x	x	x	x	x	x	x	x	x	x	x	x	x	x	x	x
Species 2	100	x	x	x	x	x	x	x	x	x	x	x	x	x	x	x	x
Species 3	94	x	x	x	x	x	x	x	x		x	x	x	x	x	x	x
Species 4	88	x	x	x	x	x	x		x	x		x	x	x	x	x	x
Species 5	81	x	x	x		x	x		x	x	x	x	x	x	x	x	
Species 6	75	x	x	x	x	x	x		x	x	x	x	x	x			
Species 7	69		x	x	x	x	x			x	x	x	x	x	x		x
Species 8	62		x		x	x	x		x	x	x		x		x	x	
Species 9	56			x	x		x		x				x	x	x	x	x
Species 10	56	x	x	x	x	x				x			x	x			x
Species 11	50					x	x	x	x			x		x	x	x	
Species 12	44		x				x	x	x				x	x	x		
Species 13	37			x	x	x				x	x			x			
Species 14	37	x	x		x					x			x		x		
Species 15	31			x	x		x								x	x	
Species 16	31			x				x	x			x	x				
Species 17	31	x	x							x			x				x
Species 18	31					x	x						x		x	x	
Species 19	25	x		x	x	x											
Species 20	25					x						x	x		x		
Species 21	25					x		x							x	x	

Species with less than 25% frequency not shown

Each of the 16 columns represents a different sample of grassy meadow vegetation dominated by Pacific wormwood and fescue. Their totality is used to define the plant community. The number of times a species is encountered in the community is calculated as a percentage of its occurrence across all 16 samples. This is shown in the "% species frequency" column.

As might be expected, Species 1 appears in every sample (100%). Other plants associated with the community appear but with less frequency. For example, Species 7 only occurs in 69 percent of the samples and Species 15 in 31 percent.

Looked at another way, if you visited this plant community, there is about a 70-percent chance of seeing Species 7, about a 30-percent chance of seeing Species 15, and a sure chance (100%) of seeing Species 1 and 2.

Frequency-ranked species lists are not available for sections 11 and higher in this guide. For these, species are listed in the order that appeared to reflect their frequency and abundance.

Species several plant communities may have in common

Few plant communities have sharp boundaries, and many of them grade into each other. Some species occur in two or more different plant communities. In this guide, shared species are generally first listed for the community in which they attain their highest percentage frequency.

Can we ignore species that occur infrequently?

For each plant community, it is the reader's choice whether to concentrate on the most frequent species or to pay equal attention to plants that occur less frequently. Some low-frequency species may be regarded as spillovers from adjacent communities, as mentioned above. However, some other low-frequency species may only be found in the plant community where they are listed, just not in every sample of it. This may include truly rare species and species of conservation concerns.

For quick acquisition of native plant knowledge, giving priority to species with 25-to-100-percent frequency in each community may be a good learning strategy, as less frequent species may still be encountered in adjacent communities.

Number of community and habitat types and their naming

This guide will take you first through the major dry belt forest types, then through the iconic Garry oak and related ecosystems, then through local wetlands and coastal shoreline habitats. In addition, it will address those native plants that are difficult to associate with the major plant communities and easily named habitats but which are of interest due to their prominence in the landscape or for their attractive appearance or other features.

The number of plant communities used in this guide has been kept as small as possible. The species combination in each named plant community may be considered significantly different from that of adjacent plant communities (compare Figure 2 on p. 24 for an overview). In the case of plant communities that contain woody plants, one or two tree species provided the most obvious name. For other plant assemblies (e.g., wetlands and shoreline vegetation), simple habitat designations were used alone or in combination. No attempt was made to either strictly follow or to supplant existing vegetation classifications.

While, for the experienced naturalist, the section headings will leave no doubt as to which plant community or habitat is being addressed, for novices the question "How do you recognize this plant community (habitat)?" is answered following each section heading.

For readers acquainted with current forestry-based ecological literature, it should be pointed out that species lists could also be derived from the subzone variant descriptions of the Coastal Douglas-fir Biogeoclimatic Zone (Green and Klinka, 1994). This guide avoids the technical terms of the biogeoclimatic classification.

Are there any intermediates between these named plant communities?

The answer is yes. There are intermediates between all plant communities that occur adjacent to each other, some more common than others, as species combinations grade into each other. To actually find the species listed under the community names used here, try to find vegetation that best fits the chosen community name.

Practical hints for observing plant communities in the field

When you enter a forest or visit any of the other communities or habitats described in this guide, focus on undisturbed portions of the native vegetation. Typically you will access the area via a road or trail. Step or face away from the trail and be aware that several of the plants that grow along the trail will not occur in the interior of the forest or other vegetation you want to observe.

This guide works best for mature examples of plant communities. Young second-growth forests, for example, will not have a complete species combination, and some species abundant in young stands will all but disappear as the forest grows older.

Accepted plant names used in this guide

Scientific and vernacular names for individual plant species in this guide follow the
BC Species and Ecosystem Explorer, a BC government website (a100.gov.bc.ca/pub/
eswp). Some previously accepted names are listed in the index with directions to the
presently accepted names.

How to use the photographs in this guide

When plants are first described, they will appear in bold text and be associated with
a hyphenated photo identification number, a scientific name and a common name.
Our sample image here is **2-19 *Calypso bulbosa* (fairy slipper)**. The number preceding the hyphen sesignates the section where the plant is introduced, and the number
following the hyphen indicates the sequence within the section, usually determined
by the plant's frequency.

You may notice that sometimes plants are mentioned in a section but no photo
of them appears. This is because they are shared with communities or habitats
described in earlier sections. The photos for these species are not repeated but may
be looked up using their section and photo identification numbers.

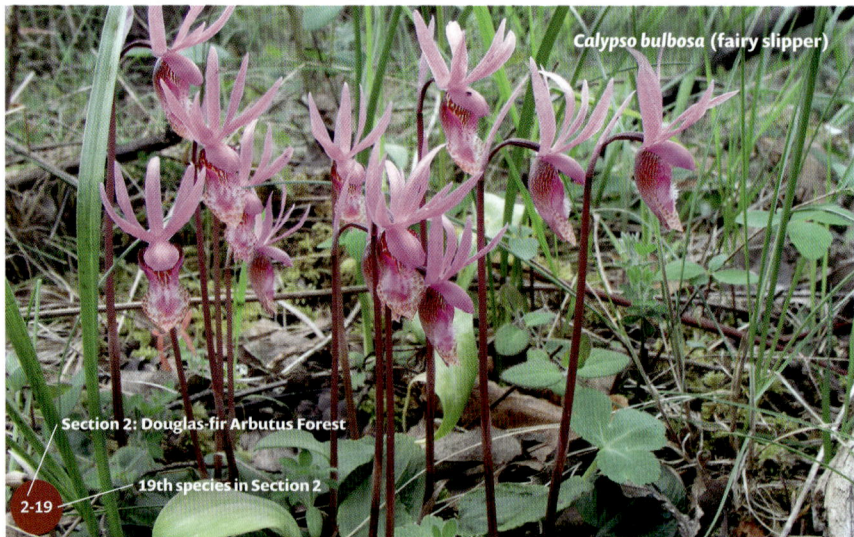

Calypso bulbosa **(fairy slipper)**

Section 2: Douglas-fir Arbutus Forest

19th species in Section 2

2-19

NATIVE PLANTS OF FOREST AND GARRY OAK ECOSYSTEMS

1   **Douglas-fir Forests**

How do you recognize these forests?

The forest will be closed (not many gaps or openings). **1-1 *Pseudotsuga menziesii* (Douglas-fir)** is always the most frequent and dominant tree. Dull Oregon-grape is the most frequent shrub. You will find these forests in places that are neither particularly wet nor dry.

The simplest expression of a well-drained Douglas-fir forest is the Douglas-fir–salal combination. Over large areas only three plant species dominate

- **1-1 *Pseudotsuga menziesii* (Douglas-fir)**
- **1-10 *Gaultheria shallon* (salal)**
- **1-32 *Kindbergia oregana* (Oregon beaked-moss)**

However, most Douglas-fir forests at low elevation and on richer soils have more species, averaging about 20.

Table 1 shows the species most likely to occur in this community. The number preceding the species name is the percentage frequency of the species in a large collection of sample stands. This is the probability of a species occurring in the sampled plant community type. It would therefore be appropriate to show only the 19 species

with the highest percentage probability of occurring. Nevertheless, more species are shown in Table 1 to account for the variability in the vegetation.

Feel free to start by selecting a manageable number of species for study, a smaller number of frequently occurring species, or a larger number including less frequently occurring species.

Table 1: Douglas-fir Forest

Tree Layer	%
Pseudotsuga menziesii (Douglas-fir)	100
Abies grandis (grand fir)	80
Thuja plicata (western redcedar)	77
Acer macrophyllum (bigleaf maple)	62
Cornus nuttallii (Pacific dogwood)	53
Taxus brevifolia (western yew)	42
Tsuga heterophylla (western hemlock)	19

Shrub Layer	%
Mahonia nervosa (dull Oregon-grape)	97
Rubus ursinus (trailing blackberry)	90
Gaultheria shallon (salal)	82
Rosa gymnocarpa (baldhip rose)	78
Vaccinium parvifolium (red huckleberry)	68
Holodiscus discolor (oceanspray)	62
Lonicera ciliosa (orange honeysuckle)	48
Frangula purshiana (cascara)	44
Symphoricarpos albus (common snowberry)	43
Symphoricarpos hesperius (trailing snowberry)	34
Amelanchier alnifolia (saskatoon)	31

Herb Layer	%
Polystichum munitum (sword fern)	88
Lysimachia latifolia (broad-leaved starflower)	87
Festuca subuliflora (crinkle-awn fescue)	65
Pteridium aquilinum (bracken fern)	64
Achlys triphylla (vanilla leaf)	59
Galium triflorum (three-flowered bedstraw)	51
Trillium ovatum (western trillium)	47
Linnaea borealis (twinflower)	45
Bromus vulgaris (Columbia brome)	33
Adenocaulon bicolor (pathfinder)	29
Melica subulata (Alaska oniongrass)	29
Monotropa uniflora (ghost pipe)	14
Corallorhiza maculata (spotted coralroot)	9

Moss Layer	%
Kindbergia oregana (Oregon beaked-moss)	98
Rhytidiadelphus triquetrus (goose-necked moss)	41
Hylocomium splendens (step moss)	40

> 75% chance of seeing this species
50–75% chance of seeing this species
25–49% chance of seeing this species
< 25% chance of seeing this species

Non-native
Ilex aquifolium (English holly)
Hedera helix (English ivy)

1-2 A more diverse Douglas-fir forest with additional tree, shrub and herbaceous species. Despite their frequent occurrence in Douglas-fir forests, the three following pictured species don't dominate the tree layer.

1-3 *Abies grandis* (grand fir).

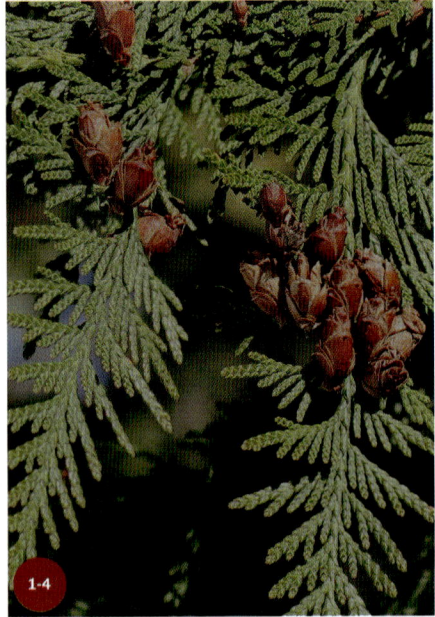

1-4 *Thuja plicata* (western redcedar).

1-5 *Taxus brevifolia* (western yew).

1-6 *Acer macrophyllum* (bigleaf maple) and **1-7 *Cornus nuttallii* (Pacific dogwood)** are deciduous trees frequently associated with Douglas-firs.

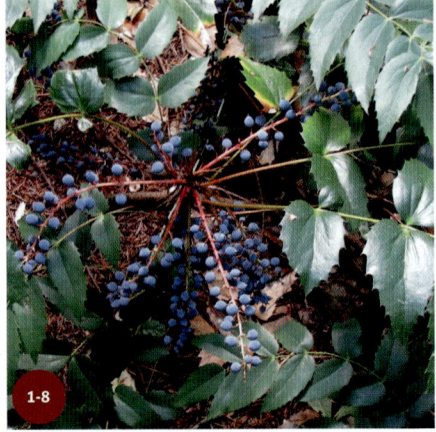

1-8 *Mahonia nervosa* (dull Oregon-grape), in flower (left) and fruit (right), is common in dry Douglas-fir forests, often in combination with *Gaultheria shallon* (salal).

1-9 *Rubus ursinus* (trailing blackberry), one of the most common shrubs on the forest floor. Fruiting is rarely seen under a closed canopy.

Like the blackberry, **1-10 *Gaultheria shallon* (salal)** is not normally seen with fruit under a closed canopy.

1-11 *Rosa gymnocarpa* **(baldhip rose)** sheds the remnants of the calyx (a whorl of green leaf-like petals at the base of the flower), hence its specific name (Greek *gymnos* = naked).

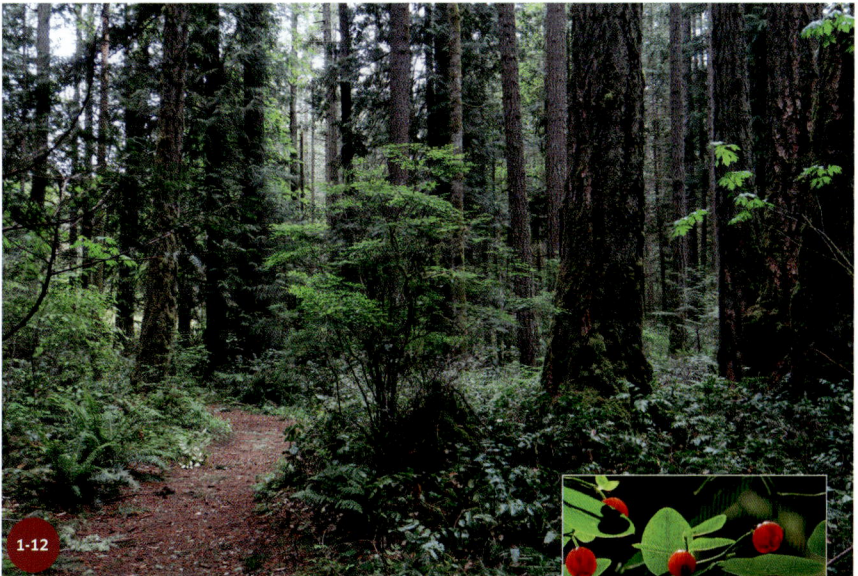

1-12 *Vaccinium parvifolium* **(red huckleberry)** shuns mineral soil. The rotten wood of old logs and stumps is its favourite habitat.

1-13
Holodiscus discolor
(oceanspray) is
a 2-to-3-metre
bush found in
dry parts of the
Douglas-fir forest.
Flowering is often
sparse under
closed canopies.

1-14 *Lonicera ciliosa*
(orange honeysuckle),
flowering (left) and
fruiting (right), is a
climbing vine. The young
shoots spiral up stems of
taller shrubs and young
trees. Non-flowering plants
can be confused with
Lonicera hispidula (hairy
honeysuckle), portrayed in
section 2, but have larger,
less leathery leaves.

1-15 *Frangula purshiana* **(cascara)**
can grow into a medium-size
tree but will never attain more
than sapling or shrub size in a
closed Douglas-fir forest. Why
then is it present in 44 percent of
all Douglas-fir forests? Cascara
berries are eaten by birds that
roost overnight in the Douglas-firs,
thereby continually re-seeding
this species with their droppings.
Small cascaras are recognized by a
fuzzy rust-coloured beak-like bud.

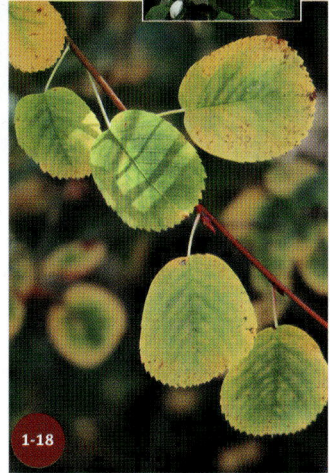

1-16 *Symphoricarpos albus* (common snowberry) is present in this and many other plant communities, usually as scattered individuals. **1-17 *Symphoricarpos hesperius* (trailing snowberry)**, when present, tends to form larger colonies and is characterized by its gracefully arching brown shoots. Like cascara, **1-18 *Amelanchier alnifolia* (saskatoon)** is also spread by berry-eating birds.

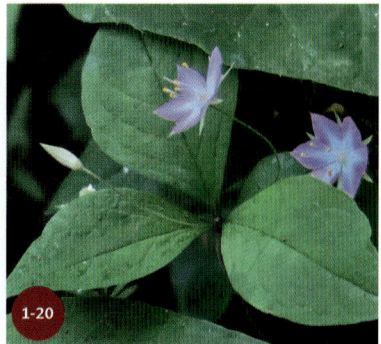

1-19 *Polystichum munitum* (sword fern) is one of the most widespread and frequent species in coastal forest communities. **1-20 *Lysimachia latifolia* (broad-leaved starflower)** is a faithful Douglas-fir associate on well-drained soils.

1-21 *Festuca subuliflora* (**crinkle-awn fescue**) is by far the most frequent grass of the Douglas-fir forest. A similar species, with a confusingly similar name, is 6-10 *Festuca subulata* (bearded fescue), found in moister environments and with a wider leaf blade.

Despite its size, **1-22** *Pteridium aquilinum* (**bracken fern**) blends in with the rest of the understory until its fall colour stands out. **1-23** *Achlys triphylla* (**vanilla leaf**), another common associate of Douglas-fir, can form large colonies.

1-24 *Galium triflorum* (**three-flowered bedstraw**) occurs in more than half of the sampled Douglas-fir stands.

1-25 *Trillium ovatum* (western trillium) is present in nearly half of all Douglas-fir forests but also occurs, usually with greater vigour, on the moist soils of mixed deciduous-coniferous forests (see Tables 3, 4 and 6).

1-26 *Linnaea borealis* (twinflower) often forms mats of several square metres at the base of large trees. The flowers are very fragrant.

1-27 *Bromus vulgaris* (Columbia brome) is a frequent grass in this forest.

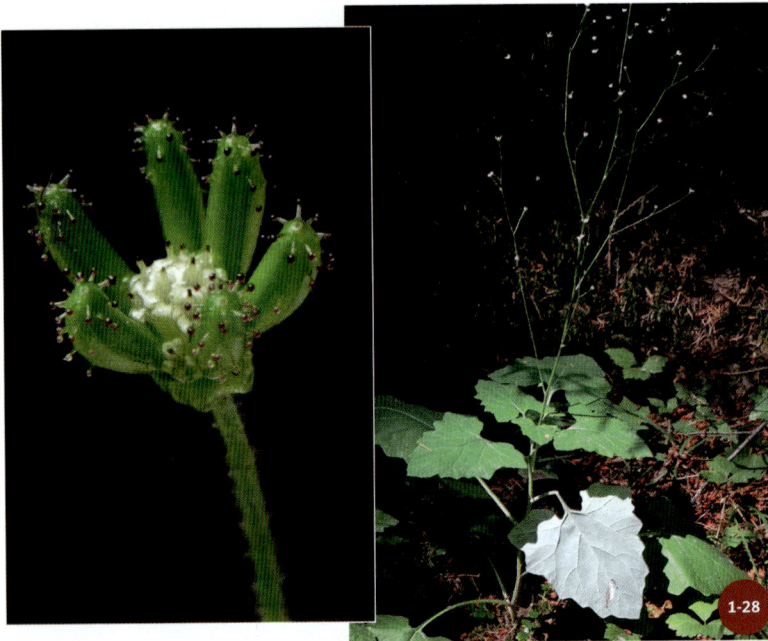

1-28 *Adenocaulon bicolor* **(pathfinder)** equips its seeds with a crown of sticky glands, enabling them to hitch a ride on the fur or clothing of passersby, thus ensuring the plant's distribution along game or hiking trails throughout the forest.

1-29 *Melica subulata* **(Alaska oniongrass)** is easily recognized by its narrow, variegated green-and-maroon spikelets, its drooping inflorescence and foliage, and its onion-like "bulb."

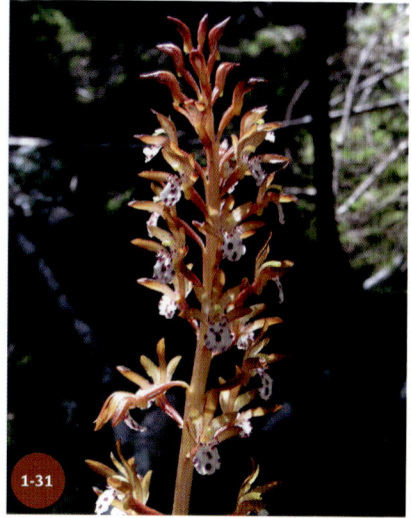

1-30 *Monotropa uniflora* **(ghost pipe)** derives its nutrition from trees via their fungal partners, thus has no need for photosynthesis. The same applies to **1-31** *Corallorhiza maculata* **(spotted coralroot)** and the less common 2-24 *Corallorhiza striata* (striped coralroot).

With 98-percent frequency, **1-32** *Kindbergia oregana* **(Oregon beaked-moss)** occurs in virtually every Douglas-fir forest. **1-33** *Rhytidiadelphus triquetrus* **(goose-necked moss)** and **1-34** *Hylocomium splendens* **(step moss)** are also common in Douglas-fir and other dry forests.

Having introduced the native plants in this most common forest type, it might be worth looking at the ecological positioning of adjacent forests (sections 2 to 6) before proceeding to the other dry belt forest communities.

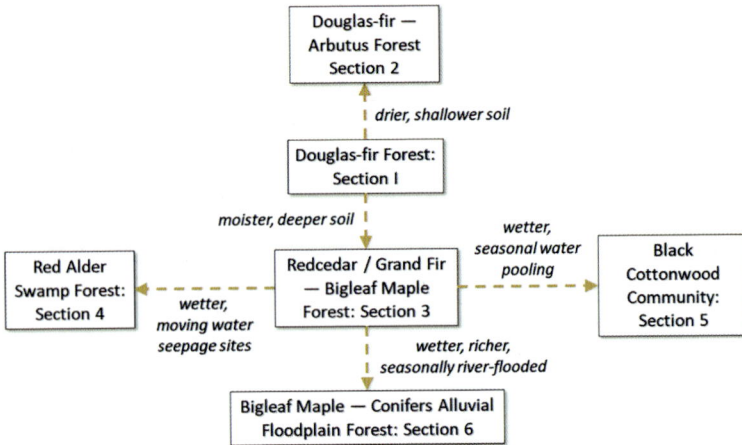

Figure 2: Moisture, soil and nutrient gradients in forest communities of the coastal dry belt.

Douglas-fir forests are the "average" or zonal vegetation of the coastal dry belt, and Douglas-fir is the tree species after which the Coastal Douglas-fir Zone is named in British Columbia's biogeoclimatic classification (Meidinger and Pojar, 1991). A Douglas-fir forest will establish itself in this area on soils that are well drained and neither too dry nor too wet.

As the zonal vegetation, the Douglas-fir forest occupies a central place in our diagram. With increases in moisture and nutrient levels, we shift from the average Douglas-fir forest to the Redcedar/Grand Fir–Bigleaf Maple combination (section 3 in this guide). If these levels increase further, we shift to the Red Alder Swamp Forest (section 4) or to the Black Cottonwood Community (section 5), depending on site hydrology.

In the other direction, if moisture levels and/or soil depth decrease, we move to the Douglas-fir–Arbutus Forest (section 2) or its higher-elevation cousin, the Shore Pine–Douglas-fir–Arbutus Woodland (section 8).

Moving in either direction away from the Douglas-fir forest, into drier or wetter environments, we experience an increased diversity and number of species. The most likely reason for this: in both directions, the amount of light that reaches the forest floor is greater and allows a larger diversity of plants to thrive.

In the wetter environments, poor soil drainage causes a larger number of trees to be up-rooted during windstorms or heavy snow events, creating gaps. In the drier environments, shallow soils alternate with bedrock outcrops that also act as gaps. These gaps receive more light, as well as having different substrates: wetter mineral soils and drier bare rock, both of which are colonized by different species.

Fitting Garry oak communities, especially Garry Oak Parklands (section 7a), into this sequence is more complicated. Their occurrence is in part determined by environmental factors and in part by anthropogenic factors, such as past management by First Nations through fire for camas and wildlife enhancement. However, Garry Oak Woodlands (section 7b) are largely similar in their moisture status to Douglas-fir–arbutus forests, except that the oak communities tend to occur on south-facing slopes, while the arbutus combination is more prevalent on other directional aspects.

Transitioning to the drier Douglas-fir–arbutus forests: **2-1 *Arbutus menziesii* (arbutus)** with flowers (inset).

2 Douglas-fir–Arbutus Forest

How do you recognize this forest?

This is a more open forest, with both Douglas-fir and arbutus present on shallow soils, often including rock outcrops, or on excessively dry gravels. Many shrub species are present, always including oceanspray.

Garry oak (7-1) is sometimes present in the (1-1) Douglas-fir–arbutus (2-1) forest. Inset photo shows the bright red-orange arbutus berries in fall.

Table 2: Douglas-fir–Arbutus Forest

Tree Layer	%
Pseudotsuga menziesii (Douglas-fir)	100
Arbutus menziesii (arbutus)	88
Quercus garryana (Garry oak)	59
Salix scouleriana (Scouler's willow)	25

Shrub Layer	%
Holodiscus discolor (oceanspray)	100
Rosa gymnocarpa (baldhip rose)	97
Rubus ursinus (trailing blackberry)	94
Symphoricarpos albus (common snowberry)	94
Mahonia aquifolium (tall Oregon-grape)	78
Lonicera ciliosa (orange honeysuckle)	78
Mahonia nervosa (dull Oregon-grape)	66
Lonicera hispidula (hairy honeysuckle)	56
Amelanchier alnifolia (saskatoon)	53
Gaultheria shallon (salal)	38
Symphoricarpos hesperius (trailing snowberry)	34
Paxistima myrsinites (falsebox)	34

Moss Layer	%
Rhytidiadelphus triquetrus (goose-necked moss)	97
Kindbergia oregana (Oregon beaked-moss)	97
Hylocomium splendens (step moss)	50
Dicranum scoparium (broom moss)	6

Non-native

Galium aparine (cleavers)

Ilex aquifolium (English holly)

Plantago lanceolata (ribwort plantain)

Vicia hirsuta (tiny vetch)

Mycelis muralis (wall lettuce)

Herb Layer	%
Bromus vulgaris (Columbia brome)	97
Moehringia macrophylla (big-leaved sandwort)	94
Melica subulata (Alaska oniongrass)	94
Sanicula crassicaulis (Pacific sanicle)	91
Lysimachia latifolia (broad-leaved starflower)	88
Erythronium oregonum (white fawn lily)	81
Festuca subuliflora (crinkle-awn fescue)	81
Lathyrus nevadensis (purple peavine)	78
Festuca occidentalis (western fescue)	72
Clinopodium douglasii (yerba buena)	63
Osmorhiza berteroi (mountain sweet-cicely)	59
Polystichum munitum (sword fern)	56
Elymus glaucus (blue wildrye)	53
Polypodium glycyrrhiza (licorice fern)	53
Goodyera oblongifolia (rattlesnake plantain)	53
Fragaria vesca (wood strawberry)	50
Hieracium albiflorum (white hawkweed)	38
Campanula scouleri (Scouler's harebell)	34
Calypso bulbosa (fairy slipper)	31
Lilium columbianum (tiger lily)	22
Anisocarpus madioides (woodland tarweed)	16
Trisetum canescens (tall trisetum)	9
Cardamine oligosperma (little western bittercress)	9
Corallorhiza striata (striped coralroot)	9
Platanthera transversa (royal rein orchid)	6

Many species of this community are shared with the Douglas-fir forest and need not be pictured again (compare 1-13 *Holodiscus discolor*, 1-11 *Rosa gymnocarpa*, 1-9 *Rubus ursinus*, 1-16 *Symphoricarpos albus*). **2-4 Mahonia aquifolium (tall Oregon-grape)** is an additional common shrub in the community.

The following shrubs are at least as frequent here as in the Douglas-fir forest: 1-14 *Lonicera ciliosa*, 1-8 *Mahonia nervosa*, 1-17 *Symphoricarpos hesperius*, 1-18 *Amelanchier alnifolia* and 1-10 *Gaultheria shallon*.

7-1 Small *Quercus garryana* (Garry oak) trees (section 7) and slender, tall **2-2 Salix scouleriana (Scouler's willow)** are additional trees in Douglas-fir–arbutus forests. The willow is barely noticeable in summer conditions but becomes conspicuous in its fall colour (2-2).

Salix scouleriana has similar leaves to 10-1 *Salix sitchensis* (Sitka willow). Scouler's willow has glabrous, often rust-coloured leaf undersides, while the Sitka willow has leaf undersides covered with dense silky hairs. Sitka willow also prefers much wetter habitats so would rarely be found side by side with Scouler's willow.

2-3 *Lonicera hispidula* **(hairy honeysuckle)** has smaller and more evergreen leaves and longer-stalked fruits than 1-14 *Lonicera ciliosa*.

2-5 *Paxistima myrsinites* **(falsebox)** is found in about one third of all stands of this community, usually near rock outcrops. The tiny maroon flowers appear early in the spring.

2-6 *Moehringia macrophylla* **(big-leaved sandwort)** occurs in nearly every stand of this community. **2-7** *Sanicula crassicaulis* **(Pacific sanicle)** is similarly common. The inset shows part of the fruiting umbel with the sticky seed burs.

Many plants frequent in the herb layer of this community are also common in the Douglas-fir forest: 1-27 *Bromus vulgaris* (Columbia brome), 1-29 *Melica subulata* (Alaska oniongrass), 1-20 *Lysimachia latifolia* (broad-leaved starflower), 1-21 *Festuca subuliflora* (crinkle-awn fescue) and 1-19 *Polystichum munitum* (sword fern).

The Douglas-fir–arbutus community is one of the principal habitats of **2-8 *Erythronium oregonum* (white fawn lily)**. The genus *Erythronium* is also known under the name "dog's tooth violets" because they have elongated tooth-shaped bulbs. **2-9 *Lathyrus nevadensis* (purple peavine)** is also a ubiquitous species in this community.

The inflorescence of **2-10 *Festuca occidentalis* (western fescue)** is similar to that of *Festuca subuliflora* (1-21). However, the low tufted leaves are narrow and thread-like, making this grass easy to recognize.

2-11 *Clinopodium douglasii* **(yerba buena)** is an aromatic herb in the mint family. Formerly known as *Satureja douglasii*, it belongs to the same genus as summer savory, an herb often used in cooking.

2-12 *Osmorhiza berteroi* **(mountain sweet-cicely)** is frequently encountered in this community but also occurs along trails in Douglas-fir forests. The sharply pointed ripe fruits are formidably barbed and easily detached into the fur of animals or clothing of people. This enables the plant to disperse over larger distances, in particular along trails.

2-13 *Elymus glaucus* (blue wildrye) is a common grass in more open habitats but makes its first appearance here, usually as a less vigorous plant than shown in this image.

2-14 *Polypodium glycyrrhiza* (licorice fern) often grows on north-facing rock walls but also on shallow soils in this community.

The leaf rosettes of the **2-15** *Goodyera oblongifolia* (rattlesnake plantain) orchid are in evidence year-round, while the hairy flowering stems come late in the summer.

2-16 *Fragaria vesca* **(wood strawberry)** is one of three local strawberries. As the name suggests, it is more frequently found in wooded areas than in open ones. Compare section 7b and section 16, where 7-38 *Fragaria virginiana* (wild strawberry) and 16-8 *Fragaria chiloensis* ssp. *pacifica* (coastal strawberry) are found.

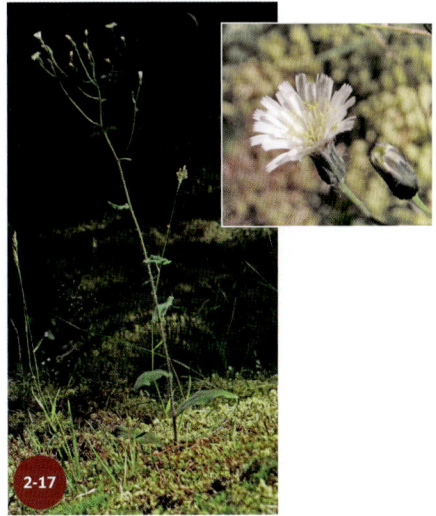

2-17 *Hieracium albiflorum* **(white hawkweed)** has hairy basal leaves and a tall stem with white dandelion-type flowers. It occurs in more than one third of all Douglas-fir–arbutus forests. The identity of non-flowering specimens of *Hieracium* can be confirmed by detaching a small part of the plant and observing the white latex juice that is common to all species in this genus.

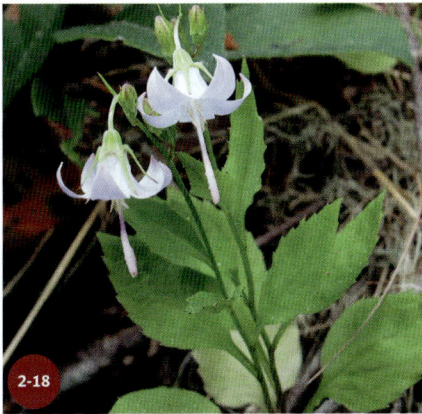

Nearly as frequent as *Hieracium* is the lovely 2-18 *Campanula scouleri* **(Scouler's harebell).**

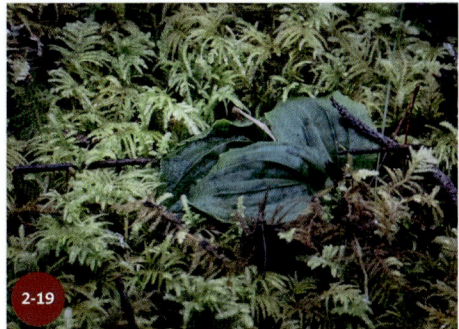

The Douglas-fir–arbutus forest is a preferred habitat for 2-19 *Calypso bulbosa* **(fairy slipper)**. The dark green ovate leaves of this orchid usually come out after the fall rains and are in evidence throughout winter.

Only a single flower of **2-20** *Lilium columbianum* **(tiger lily)** is shown here, but this is a tall plant, often with several flowers where it receives more light.

2-21 *Anisocarpus madioides* **(woodland tarweed)** grows from a slender tall stem. Its lower leaves are much larger than its upper ones.

2-22 *Cardamine oligosperma* **(little western bittercress)** occurs in well-lit mossy openings in this community and the oak woodlands. Without detailed examination, it is indistinguishable from the introduced *Cardamine hirsuta*, which can often be found in similar places.

2-23 *Trisetum canescens* **(tall trisetum)** is an uncommon grass found mainly in this community. Unlike most other forest grasses, it bears its inflorescence straight up.

2-24 *Corallorhiza striata* **(striped coralroot)** is a showier sister of the spotted coralroot (1-31).

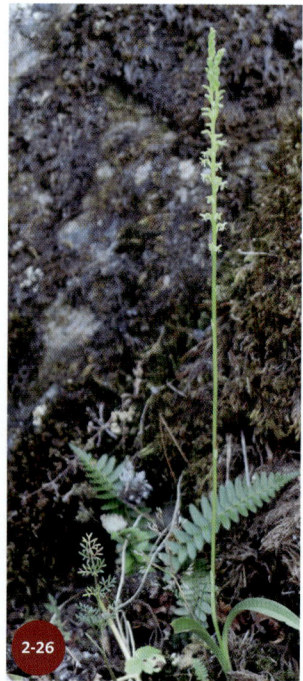

Like all rein orchids, **2-25 *Platanthera transversa* (royal rein orchid)** and **2-26 *Platanthera unalascensis* (Alaska rein orchid)** are likely to puzzle the observer, as the leaves and the flowering stems are rarely found at the same time. The leaves of these two orchids, which are near identical, emerge very early in the spring; flowering occurs in early summer, when the basal leaves have withered. Both species are occasionally found in this community. *Platanthera transversa* has long, horizontally held spurs, while *Platanthera unalascensis* has short, downward-curved spurs. The latter also differs by being sweetly scented.

The moss layer in the Douglas-fir–arbutus forest is identical with that of the Douglas-fir forest and consists of 1-32 *Kindbergia oregana* (Oregon beaked-moss), 1-33 *Rhytidiadelphus triquetrus* (goose-necked moss) and 1-34 *Hylocomium splendens* (step moss). *Dicranum scoparium* (broom moss) is an addition on open rock outcrops and will be featured in section 8.

Redcedar/Grand Fir–Bigleaf Maple Forest

How do you recognize this forest?

The three species mentioned in the heading have near-equal shares in the tree layer, but Douglas-firs are sometimes present. Sword ferns are usually prominent on the forest floor.

The image above shows a mature example of this forest. As usual, the maple trunks (1-6 *Acer macrophyllum*) are covered with mosses, liverworts and, in part, with epiphytic licorice ferns (2-14 *Polypodium glycyrrhiza*).

A single red alder (4-1 *Alnus rubra*, leaning) is left from an earlier, more open successional stage. Conifers are grand fir (1-3 *Abies grandis*, centre) and western redcedar (1-4 *Thuja plicata*).

The forest occurs on flat or gently sloping ground at low elevations and on rich loamy soils or marine clay. Imperfect drainage results in more overturned trees and enhances diversity in the herbaceous ground vegetation. Mature examples of this community are rare because their rich soils have long been converted to agricultural land.

Table 3: Redcedar/Grand Fir–Bigleaf Maple Forest

Tree Layer	%
Acer macrophyllum (bigleaf maple)	96
Thuja plicata (western redcedar)	92
Alnus rubra (red alder)	88
Abies grandis (grand fir)	80
Frangula purshiana (cascara)	44
Pseudotsuga menziesii (Douglas-fir)	28

Shrub Layer	%
Oemleria cerasiformis (osoberry)	92
Rubus ursinus (trailing blackberry)	84
Symphoricarpos albus (common snowberry)	80
Ribes divaricatum (wild black gooseberry)	64
Sambucus racemosa var. *arborescens* (coastal red elderberry)	52
Rubus spectabilis (salmonberry)	52
Holodiscus discolor (oceanspray)	28
Vaccinium parvifolium (red huckleberry)	24

Moss Layer	%
Kindbergia praelonga (slender beaked-moss)	88
Plagiomnium insigne (coastal leafy moss)	84
Leucolepis acanthoneuron (Menzies' tree moss)	68
Kindbergia oregana (Oregon beaked-moss)	40

Herb Layer	%
Polystichum munitum (sword fern)	100
Tiarella trifoliata var. *trifoliata* (three-leaved foamflower)	92
Trillium ovatum (western trillium)	68
Tellima grandiflora (fringecup)	64
Dryopteris expansa (spiny wood fern)	48
Galium triflorum (three-flowered bedstraw)	48
Claytonia sibirica (Siberian miner's-lettuce)	44
Carex leptopoda (short-scaled sedge)	44
Ranunculus uncinatus (little buttercup)	24
Osmorhiza berteroi (mountain sweet-cicely)	24
Stellaria crispa (crisp starwort)	20
Carex hendersonii (Henderson's sedge)	20

Non-native
Mycelis muralis (wall lettuce)
Ilex aquifolium (English holly)
Poa trivialis (common bluegrass)
Stellaria media (common chickweed)
Galium aparine (cleavers)

> 75% chance of seeing this species
50–75% chance of seeing this species
25–49% chance of seeing this species
< 25% chance of seeing this species

Similar species combinations are also found in a narrow transitional belt between well-drained conifer forests and wetter sites occupied by red alder or black cottonwood (*Populus trichocarpa*).

This forest type is variable and can have scattered taller shrubs such as salmonberry (3-4 *Rubus spectabilis*), wild black gooseberry (3-2 *Ribes divaricatum*), coastal red elderberry (3-3 *Sambucus racemosa* var. *arborescens*) and osoberry (3-1 *Oemleria cerasiformis*), in addition to common snowberry (1-16 *Symphoricarpos albus*) and trailing blackberry (1-9 *Rubus ursinus*).

Osoberry (3-1 *Oemleria cerasiformis*), salmonberry (3-4 *Rubus spectabilis*) and coastal red elderberry (3-3 *Sambucus racemosa* var. *arborescens*) all flower early in the year and have vividly coloured fruit by early summer. All these shrubs occur in 50 percent or more of the stands sampled in this community, while oceanspray (1-13 *Holodiscus discolor*) and red huckleberry (1-12 *Vaccinium parvifolium*) are less common.

Fruiting *Sambucus racemosa* var. *arborescens*.

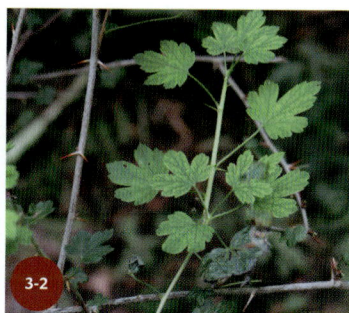

While never present in large numbers, **wild black gooseberry** (**3-2** *Ribes divaricatum*) is a characteristic species in this forest. It also occurs sporadically in wetter forests and swamps, such as the black cottonwood forest and alder swamps.

1-19 *Polystichum munitum* (sword fern) occurs in all forest communities of our region. However, it reaches its highest frequency of occurrence (100%) and its greatest vigour in these forests. 1-25 *Trillium ovatum* (western trillium) also benefits from greater moisture levels in this forest type.

3-5 *Tiarella trifoliata* **var.** *trifoliata* **(three-leaved foamflower) is** another ubiquitous species in this and other moist habitats.

3-6 *Tellima grandiflora* **(fringecup)** makes its first appearance here but reaches its best development in red alder swamps (section 4).

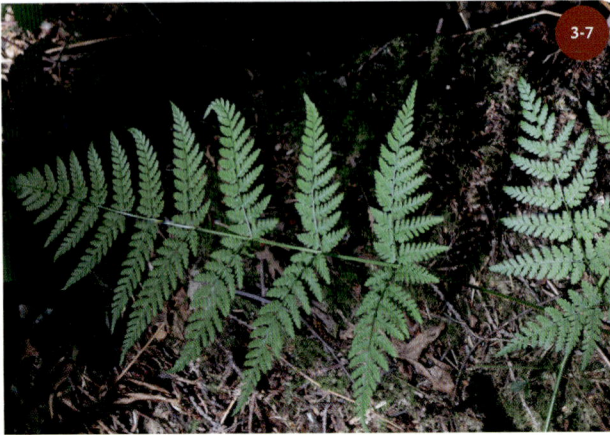

3-7 Dryopteris expansa (spiny wood fern) has a triangular outline, with its longest pinnae at the base of the frond, whereas the fronds of 4-5 *Athyrium filix-femina* (lady fern) are broadest at mid-length and narrow toward both the tip and the base.

1-24 *Galium triflorum* (three-flowered bedstraw) and 2-12 *Osmorhiza berteroi* (mountain sweet-cicely) are shared with drier forest habitats.

3-8 Claytonia sibirica (Siberian miner's-lettuce) and **3-9 Carex leptopoda (short-scaled sedge)** occur in nearly half of the stands of this forest, while the frequency of the next two species is just under 25 percent.

3-10 *Ranunculus uncinatus* **(little buttercup)** and **3-11** *Stellaria crispa* **(crisp starwort)** take advantage of slightly better lit yet moist micro-habitats in this forest type.

3-12 *Carex hendersonii* **(Henderson's sedge)** is easily distinguished by its wide leaves and a few-flowered spike.

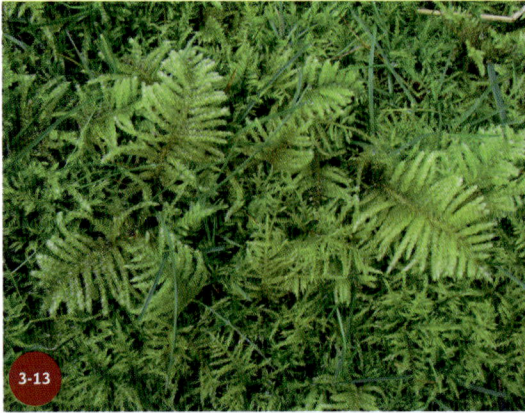

Both **3-13 *Kindbergia praelonga* (slender beaked-moss)** and its bigger sister 1-32 *Kindbergia oregana* (Oregon beaked-moss) are shown in the same photo. Our image of **3-14 *Plagiomnium insigne* (coastal leafy moss)** shows it surrounded by *Kindbergia praelonga*. The adjacent picture shows the coastal leafy moss with emerging sporophytes.

3-15 *Leucolepis acanthoneuron* (Menzies' tree moss) is another frequent moss in the Redcedar/Grand fir–Bigleaf maple forest. The bright green "crowns" of this palm tree-like species are the current season's shoots, while the dull green crowns, including the sporophytes, are from the previous season.

4 Red Alder Swamp Forest

How do you recognize this forest?

The characteristic feature of this forest is year-round wet ground, derived from slope seepage and springs rather than flooding. Early developmental stages are a combination of red alder and skunk cabbage. Later stages have redcedar, western hemlock and sometimes Sitka spruce. Giant horsetail is common.

The image above shows this swamp community in a young successional stage with
4-6 *Lysichiton americanus* **(skunk cabbage)** dominating the ground vegetation under
4-1 *Alnus rubra* **(red alder)**.

1-6 *Acer macrophyllum* (bigleaf maple) and 1-15 *Frangula purshiana* (cascara) are present in half or more of the stands.

The shrub layer in this community is dominated by 3-4 *Rubus spectabilis* (salmonberry), but 3-1 *Oemleria cerasiformis* (osoberry), 3-3 *Sambucus racemosa* var. *arborescens* (coastal red elderberry), 1-9 *Rubus ursinus* (trailing blackberry) and 1-12 *Vaccinium parvifolium* (red huckleberry) are also present in suitable micro-habitats.

Table 4: Red Alder Swamp Forest

Tree Layer	%
Thuja plicata (western redcedar)	97
Alnus rubra (red alder)	92
Acer macrophyllum (bigleaf maple)	53
Frangula purshiana (cascara)	50
Tsuga heterophylla (western hemlock)	35
Picea sitchensis (Sitka spruce)	21

Shrub Layer	%
Rubus spectabilis (salmonberry)	96
Oemleria cerasiformis (osoberry)	85
Sambucus racemosa var. *arborescens* (coastal red elderberry)	78
Rubus ursinus (trailing blackberry)	54
Vaccinium parvifolium (red huckleberry)	44
Ribes bracteosum (stink currant)	35

Moss Layer	%
Kindbergia praelonga (slender goosenecked moss)	94
Plagiomnium insigne (coastal leafy moss)	90
Leucolepis acanthoneuron (Menzies' tree moss)	71
Rhizomnium glabrescens (large leafy moss)	36
Brachythecium sp. (brachythecium moss)	33
Kindbergia oregana (Oregon beaked-moss)	28
Plagiochila porelloides (cedar shake liverwort)	19
Buckiella undulata (flat-moss)	17

Non-native
Mycelis muralis (wall lettuce)
Ilex aquifolium (English holly)

Herb Layer	%
Athyrium filix-femina (lady fern)	99
Lysichiton americanus (skunk cabbage)	96
Polystichum munitum (sword fern)	90
Tiarella trifoliata var. *trifoliata* (three-leaved foamflower)	89
Stachys chamissonis var. *cooleyae* (Cooley's hedge-nettle)	76
Equisetum telmateia (giant horsetail)	75
Maianthemum dilatatum (false lily-of-the-valley)	74
Dryopteris expansa (spiny wood fern)	71
Streptopus amplexifolius (clasping twistedstalk)	69
Trillium ovatum (western trillium)	61
Claytonia sibirica (Siberian miner's-lettuce)	57
Carex leptopoda (short-scaled sedge)	47
Galium triflorum (three-flowered bedstraw)	47
Tellima grandiflora (fringecup)	38
Angelica genuflexa (kneeling angelica)	28
Urtica dioica (stinging nettle)	21
Cardamine occidentalis (western bittercress)	18
Oenanthe sarmentosa (Pacific water-parsley)	17
Platanthera stricta (slender bog orchid)	17
Torreyochloa pallida var. *pauciflora* (weak false-manna)	13
Cinna latifolia (nodding wood-reed)	11

> 75% chance of seeing this species
50–75% chance of seeing this species
25–49% chance of seeing this species
< 25% chance of seeing this species

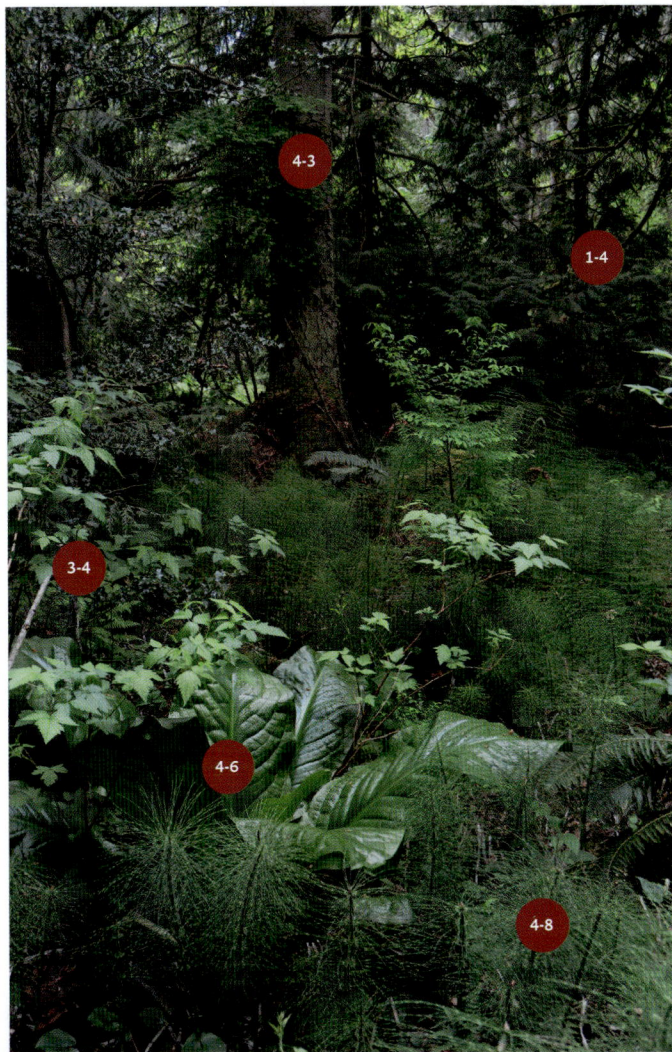

This image shows a more advanced stage in this community, after conifers have gained a foothold among the alders.

After enough decaying wood and litter have accumulated, 1-4 *Thuja plicata* (western redcedar), **4-2 *Tsuga heterophylla* (western hemlock)** and, rarely, even **4-3 *Picea sitchensis* (Sitka spruce)** become established. The advanced stage with Sitka spruce (as pictured on this page) is now quite rare in the dry belt because most of its habitat has been drained and cleared for agriculture.

Alnus rubra (red alder) swamp forests are uncommon in our landscape because they depend on moving ground water such as large-scale toe-slope seepage or natural springs. Successionally advanced examples of this plant community (where conifers have gained a foothold) are now rare due to drainage and agriculture. The same applies to the *Populus trichocarpa* (black cottonwood) community type, which occupies equally wet ground but does not depend on springs and seepage. It occurs in flat areas or depressions subject to flooding but tolerates more stagnant or seasonally fluctuating water tables.

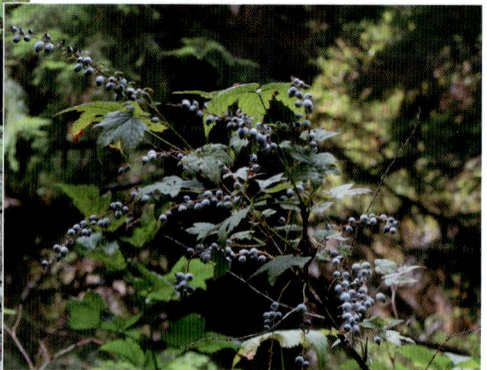

4-4 *Ribes bracteosum* (stink currant) occurs in more than a third of red alder swamps.

In the herb layer **4-5 *Athyrium filix-femina* (lady fern), 4-6 *Lysichiton americanus* (skunk cabbage), 4-7 *Stachys chamissonis* var. *cooleyae* (Cooley's hedge-nettle)** and **4-8 *Equisetum telmateia* (giant horsetail)** are present in more than 75 percent of all red alder swamp forests, as are 1-19 *Polystichum munitum* (sword fern) and 3-5 *Tiarella trifoliata* var. *trifoliata* (three-leaved foamflower).

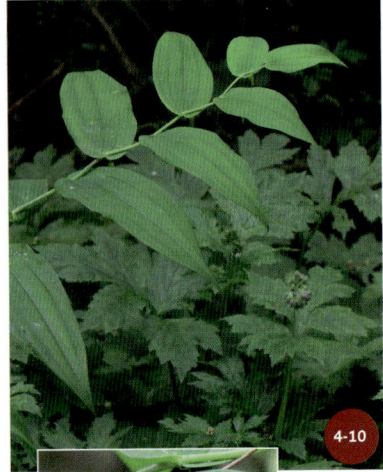

4-9 *Maianthemum dilatatum*
(false lily-of-the-valley), 3-7 *Dryopteris*
expansa (spiny wood fern), **4-10 Streptopus**
***amplexifolius* (clasping twistedstalk),**
1-25 *Trillium ovatum* (western trillium) and
3-8 *Claytonia sibirica* (Siberian miner's-
lettuce) occur in more than 50 percent of
the stands of this species-rich community.

Three species known to us from other moist forests
occur in more than one third of the swamp stands:
3-9 *Carex leptopoda* (short-scaled sedge), 1-24 *Galium*
triflorum (three-flowered bedstraw) and 3-6 *Tellima*
grandiflora (fringecup). Less common are the
following: **4-11 Urtica dioica (stinging nettle), 4-12**
***Cardamine pensylvanica* (Pennsylvanian bittercress)**
and the similar *Cardamine occidentalis* (western
bittercress, not pictured).

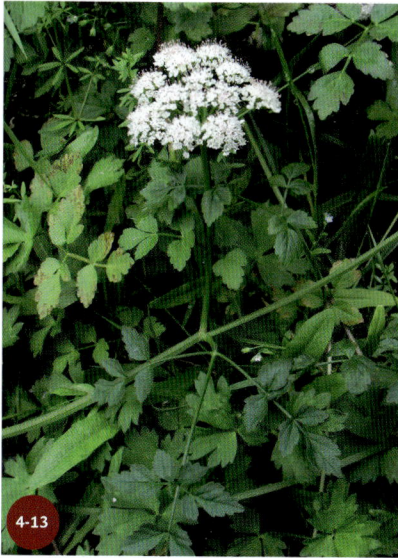

The white-flowered **4-13 *Oenanthe sarmentosa* (Pacific water-parsley)** grows partly submerged in seepage rivulets and puddles and is shared with other wet forests and swamps.

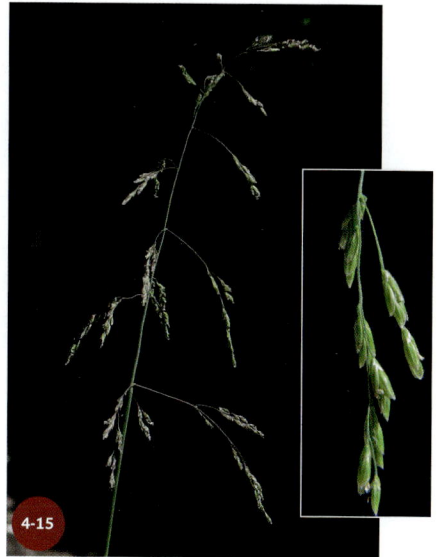

4-15 *Torreyochloa pallida* var. *pauciflora* (weak false-manna) is another grass found in muddy depressions here and in other wet plant communities. Its spikelets resemble those of *Glyceria* (mannagrass) species, but it has lax broad leaves tapering to a thin point.

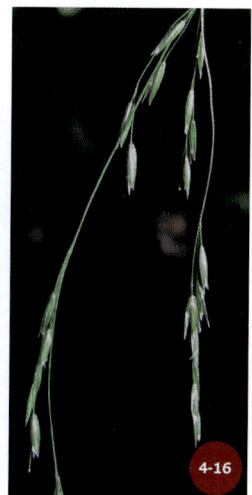

4-14 *Platanthera stricta* (slender bog orchid) and **4-16 *Cinna latifolia* (nodding wood-reed)** are mainly in successionally advanced swamp forests and are locally uncommon.

The most frequent mosses are 3-13 *Kindbergia praelonga* (slender beaked-moss), 3-14 *Plagiomnium insigne* (coastal leafy moss) and 3-15 *Leucolepis acanthoneuron* (Menzies' tree moss). Among the liverworts, the pretty **4-19 Plagiochila porelloides (cedar shake liverwort)** is prominent. **4-17 Rhizomnium glabrescens (large leafy moss)** and **4-20 Buckiella undulata (flat-moss)** come in under increasing conifer cover. **4-18 Brachythecium sp. (brachythecium moss)** usually forms sterile mats.

Red alders in winter.

5 Black Cottonwood Community

How do you recognize this community?

As a result of water pooling and flooding, this community is wet from fall to late spring but may become dry in late summer. This is a broad-leaved community with an occasional grand fir mixed in. The *Populus trichocarpa* community is characterized by three main dominants: the eponymous **5-1 *Populus trichocarpa* (black cottonwood)** in the tree layer, **5-3 *Cornus sericea* (red-osier dogwood)** in the shrub layer and **5-11 *Carex obnupta* (slough sedge)** in the herb layer.

As shown in Table 5, sword fern and short-scaled sedge occur in more stands than slough sedge, but as scattered individuals rather than the solid ground cover formed by 5-11 *Carex obnupta* (slough sedge).

In the tree layer, several species familiar from previous sections may occur as associates. A new tree species occasionally found in this community is **5-2 *Populus tremuloides* (trembling aspen)**.

Shrubs already encountered in other forests include 1-9 *Rubus ursinus* (trailing blackberry), 3-1 *Oemleria cerasiformis* (osoberry), 1-16 *Symphoricarpos albus* (common snowberry) and 3-2 *Ribes divaricatum* (wild black gooseberry).

Despite the seasonally changing wet ground conditions, many different shrubs rarely found in other native habitats can be associated with this community. The reason for this diversity becomes clear when one considers that in precolonial times such wet habitats formed the few breaks where light-loving species could thrive in the surrounding shady closed-canopy conifer forests.

The herb layers in the *Populus trichocarpa* and red alder swamp communities exhibit species overlap. Shared species include 1-19 *Polystichum munitum*, 3-9 *Carex leptopoda*, 4-9 *Maianthemum dilatatum*, 4-7 *Stachys chamissonis* var. *cooleyae*, 3-6 *Tellima grandiflora* and 4-13 *Oenanthe sarmentosa*.

Table 5: Black Cottonwood Community

Tree Layer	%
Populus trichocarpa (black cottonwood)	90
Abies grandis (grand fir)	76
Frangula purshiana (cascara)	69
Alnus rubra (red alder)	59
Acer macrophyllum (bigleaf maple)	24
Populus tremuloides (trembling aspen)	17

Shrub Layer	%
Cornus sericea (red-osier dogwood)	97
Rubus ursinus (trailing blackberry)	93
Oemleria cerasiformis (osoberry)	83
Malus fusca (Pacific crab apple)	83
Symphoricarpos albus (common snowberry)	79
Lonicera involucrata (black twinberry)	48
Rosa nutkana (Nootka rose)	38
Ribes divaricatum (wild black gooseberry)	31
Physocarpus capitatus (Pacific ninebark)	21
Spiraea douglasii (hardhack)	21
Rosa pisocarpa (clustered wild rose)	17
Crataegus douglasii (black hawthorn)	14

Herb Layer	%
Polystichum munitum (sword fern)	86
Carex leptopoda (short-scaled sedge)	79
Carex obnupta (slough sedge)	66
Maianthemum dilatatum (false lily-of-the-valley)	52
Stachys chamissonis var. *cooleyae* (Cooley's hedge-nettle)	48
Tellima grandiflora (fringecup)	41
Oenanthe sarmentosa (Pacific water-parsley)	34
Equisetum hyemale (scouring rush)	21

Moss Layer	%
Kindbergia praelonga (slender beaked-moss)	90
Leucolepis acanthoneuron (Menzies' tree moss)	55
Plagiomnium insigne (coastal leafy moss)	31
Brachythecium sp. (brachythecium moss)	24

Non-native
Poa trivialis (common bluegrass)
Mycelis muralis (wall lettuce)
Rumex obtusifolius (bitter dock)
Galium aparine (cleavers)
Ilex aquifolium (English holly)
Agrostis gigantea (redtop)
Ranunculus repens (creeping buttercup)

> 75% chance of seeing this species
50–75% chance of seeing this species
25–49% chance of seeing this species
< 25% chance of seeing this species

As well as the dominant **5-3 *Cornus sericea* (red-osier dogwood)**, **5-4 *Malus fusca* (Pacific crab apple)** occurs in most stands of this community. In about half of the stands, we find **5-5 *Lonicera involucrata* (black twinberry)**, **5-6 *Rosa nutkana* (Nootka rose)**. Less frequent are **5-7 *Physocarpus capitatus* (Pacific ninebark)**, **5-8 *Spiraea douglasii* (hardhack)**, **5-9 *Rosa pisocarpa* (clustered wild rose)** and **5-10 *Crataegus douglasii* (black hawthorn)**.

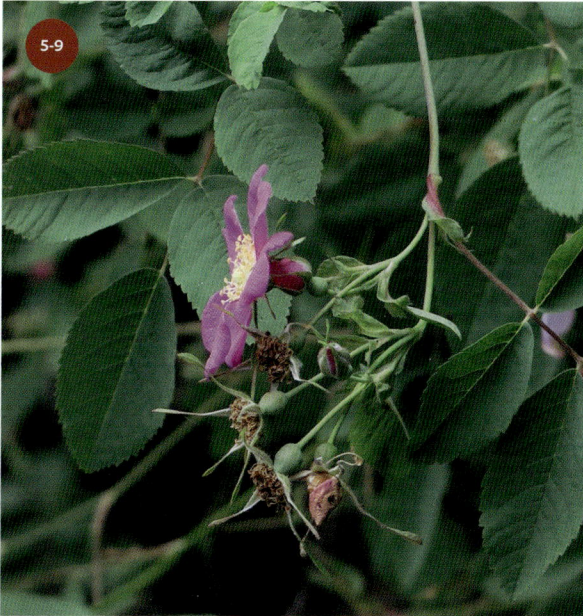

5-9 *Rosa pisocarpa* (clustered wild rose) is distinguished from the more common 5-6 *Rosa nutkana* by being smaller and more delicate in all its parts. Its flowers and fruits are clustered in threes or more.

5-10 *Crataegus douglasii* (black hawthorn) is distinguished from the introduced European hawthorn by its black (rather than red) fruits and by less lobed leaves and large thorns.

5-11 *Carex obnupta* (slough sedge) flowers in April. The black female spikes, now with white stigmas, will be drooping later in the season, while the brown male spikes, now with yellow anthers, will remain upright.

5-12 *Equisetum hyemale* (scouring rush) is restricted to the cottonwood community. This horsetail (not a rush in the botanical sense!) was used by Indigenous peoples to smooth wooden implements (N. Turner, p.c., 2023) and by European settlers for scouring pots, hence the common name.

Species in the moss layer of the *Populus trichocarpa* community are shared with red alder swamps: 3-13 *Kindbergia praelonga*, 3-15 *Leucolepis acanthoneuron*, 3-14 *Plagiomnium insigne* and 4-18 *Brachythecium* species.

6 Bigleaf Maple–Conifers Alluvial Floodplain Forest

How do you recognize this forest?

It is always located along the banks of rivers and in its original form (now rare) contains all large trees of the region. The very rich shrub layer usually includes salmonberry, and the equally rich herb layer always contains sword fern.

This forest type is most similar to the plant community described under section 3, the Redcedar/Grand Fir–Bigleaf Maple Forest. It is described here because, on the one hand, it unites many species also encountered in the two preceding plant communities (sections 4 and 5) and, on the other hand, contains several species not normally found in the dry belt.

The forests of section 3 have richer and more moisture-retentive soils than the well-drained Douglas-fir forests (section 1). Alluvial floodplain forests have even richer soils due to the input of new sediments by periodic flooding. Moreover, the coarser-textured sandy-gravelly substrates provide better aeration and drainage when

Table 6: Bigleaf Maple–Conifers Alluvial Floodplain Forest

Tree Layer	%
Acer macrophyllum (bigleaf maple)	100
Thuja plicata (western redcedar)	95
Abies grandis (grand fir)	59
Tsuga heterophylla (western hemlock)	55
Alnus rubra (red alder)	36
Pseudotsuga menziesii (Douglas-fir)	32
Picea sitchensis (Sitka spruce)	10
Populus trichocarpa (black cottonwood)	10

Moss Layer	%
Kindbergia praelonga (slender beaked-moss)	100
Leucolepis acanthoneuron (Menzies' tree moss)	73
Plagiomnium insigne (coastal leafy moss)	73
Kindbergia oregana (Oregon beaked-moss)	68
Brachythecium sp. (brachythecium moss)	36
Rhytidiadelphus triquetrus (goose-necked moss)	36
Hylocomium splendens (step moss)	14
Rhytidiadelphus loreus (lanky moss)	14

Shrub Layer	%
Rubus ursinus (trailing blackberry)	91
Rubus spectabilis (salmonberry)	87
Symphoricarpos albus (common snowberry)	87
Oemleria cerasiformis (osoberry)	68
Sambucus racemosa var. *arborescens* (coastal red elderberry)	41
Mahonia nervosa (dull Oregon-grape)	32
Rubus parviflorus (thimbleberry)	32
Corylus cornuta ssp. *californica* (beaked hazelnut)	27
Oplopanax horridus (devil's club)	27
Ribes bracteosum (stink currant)	27
Vaccinium parvifolium (red huckleberry)	27
Cornus sericea (red-osier dogwood)	14
Acer glabrum (Douglas maple)	10
Mahonia aquifolium (tall Oregon-grape)	10

Herb Layer	%
Polystichum munitum (sword fern)	100
Prosartes hookeri (Hooker's fairybells)	87
Athyrium filix-femina (lady fern)	83
Bromus vulgaris (Columbia brome)	83
Carex leptopoda (short-scaled sedge)	83
Tiarella trifoliata var. *trifoliata* (three-leaved foamflower)	70
Carex hendersonii (Henderson's sedge)	68
Tellima grandiflora (fringecup)	68
Achlys triphylla (vanilla leaf)	55
Maianthemum dilatatum (false lily-of-the-valley)	55
Stachys chamissonis var. *cooleyae* (Cooley's hedge-nettle)	55
Ranunculus uncinatus (little buttercup)	46
Dryopteris expansa (spiny wood fern)	41
Dicentra formosa ssp. *formosa* (Pacific bleeding heart)	41
Adenocaulon bicolor (pathfinder)	36
Adiantum aleuticum (western maidenhair fern)	36
Galium triflorum (three-flowered bedstraw)	36
Lysimachia latifolia (broad-leaved starflower)	36
Tolmiea menziesii (piggy-back plant)	32

Herb Layer	%
Osmorhiza berteroi (mountain sweet-cicely)	28
Thalictrum occidentale (western meadowrue)	27
Urtica dioica (stinging nettle)	27
Equisetum telmateia (giant horsetail)	23
Trillium ovatum (western trillium)	23
Equisetum hyemale (scouring rush)	18
Festuca subulata (bearded fescue)	18
Festuca subuliflora (crinkle-awned fescue)	18
Hydrophyllum tenuipes (Pacific waterleaf)	18
Pectiantia ovalis (oval-leaved mitrewort)	18
Pteridium aquilinum (bracken fern)	18
Gymnocarpium disjunctum (western oak fern)	14
Trautvetteria caroliniensis (false bugbane)	14
Viola glabella (stream violet)	14
Heracleum maximum (cow parsnip)	10
Luzula parviflora (small-flowered woodrush)	10
Poa marcida (weeping bluegrass)	10
Tiarella trifoliata var. *laciniata* (cut-leaved foamflower)	10

Non-native
Geranium robertianum (herb-Robert)
Mycelis muralis (wall lettuce)
Ilex aquifolium (English holly)
Alliaria petiolata (garlic mustard)

> 75% chance of seeing this species
50–75% chance of seeing this species
25–49% chance of seeing this species
< 25% chance of seeing this species

they are not flooded. Moisture-loving species also benefit because the water table is normally within reach.

Alluvial floodplain forests in general have the highest plant species diversity among all closed forests, and ours make no exception. They have more species than our other forests, and that is true for each of the layers: trees, shrubs, herbs and bryophytes. In unaltered examples, the height and diameter of almost all tree species is the greatest among all forest communities of the dry belt.

Unfortunately, all these superlatives amount to an epitaph for what little remains of these once magnificent forests. The frequencies in Table 6 are based on 22 sample lists from eight localities on the dry east side of Vancouver Island. Of 14 river floodplains in the dry belt, six had no acceptable fragments of this forest type left, and imperfect examples had to be included when sampling in all the others.

Destruction of alluvial floodplain forests started early in the colonial history of the dry belt region, not only because of their high timber values, but also because their flat topography and rich soils made excellent farmland. More recently, myriad industrial and residential land uses—as well as associated drainage and flood control installations—continue to take their toll.

In the tree layer of these forests, 1-4 *Thuja plicata* (western redcedar) and 1-6 *Acer macrophyllum* (bigleaf maple) are always present and dominant. They are usually combined with other tree species familiar to us from sections 1, 3, 4 and 5.

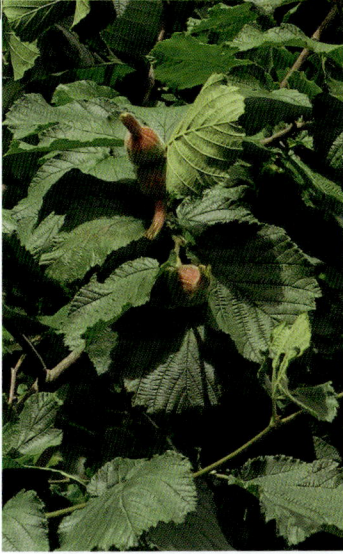

In the shrub layer, the dominant and high-frequency species are also well known from preceding sections, with 3-4 *Rubus spectabilis* (salmonberry) often the most conspicuous. It is the occasional occurrences of new species that sets this forest type apart: **6-1 *Rubus parviflorus* (thimbleberry)**, while not unknown in other, often disturbed habitats, finds its home here; **6-2 *Corylus cornuta* ssp. *californica* (beaked hazelnut)** is also new, though it is restricted to the southern part of our region.

This forest type is also the only one in our coastal dry belt where **6-3 *Oplopanax horridus* (devil's club)** makes a showing, usually in the lushest parts. **6-4 *Acer glabrum* (Douglas maple)** is a tall shrub or a small tree that prefers the gravelly substrates common in the floodplain habitat.

The luxuriant and species-rich herb layer of this forest is home to most of the additional species among the many herbs, grasses and sedges that we have encountered in several of the preceding sections.

**6-4 *Acer glabrum*
(Douglas maple).**

6-5 *Prosartes hookeri* (Hooker's fairybells)
is the most frequent species after
1-19 *Polystichum munitum* (sword fern). *P. hookeri* is a member of the lily family. It flowers in late spring, with delicate white flowers hanging down below parallel-veined leaves. The plant bears yellow or red twinned berries in the summer.

6-6 *Dicentra formosa* ssp. *formosa* (Pacific bleeding heart) is a member of the poppy family. This is one of our more attractive wildflowers, which is reflected in the specific name *formosa* ("handsome").

6-7 *Adiantum aleuticum* (western maidenhair fern), with its graceful fan shape, black stems, and midribs that contrast with the bright green pinnules, may be our most beautiful fern.

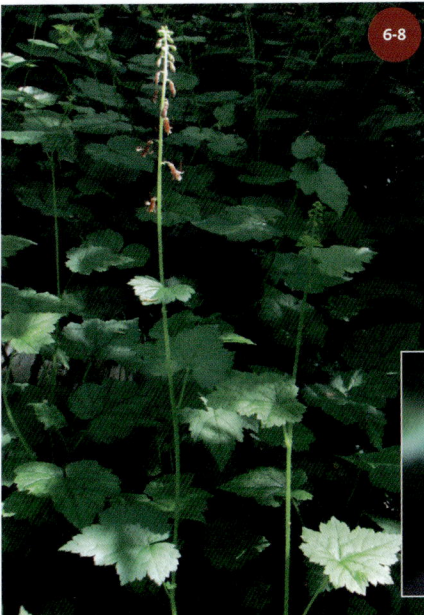

6-8 *Tolmiea menziesii* (piggy-back plant or youth-on-age) derives its common names from the fact that young plantlets develop on top of older leaves, attached to the leaf axils. This is a member of the saxifrage family, but you wouldn't guess it from the highly asymmetrical flowers. The four threads emanating from the flowering tube in our photograph are actually the petals!

6-9 *Thalictrum occidentale* (western meadowrue) bears male and female flowers on separate plants. Here the pistillate (female) flowers are shown on the left and the staminate (male) flowers above. Neither male nor female flowers have petals in this 50-to-100-centimetre-tall member of the buttercup family.

6-10 *Festuca subulata* (bearded fescue) is the less common of the two similar fescues, *F. subuliflora* and *F. subulata*. Apart from the microscopic flowering feature, the latter has wider leaves that are nearly hairless, while the former has a pubescent upper leaf surface.

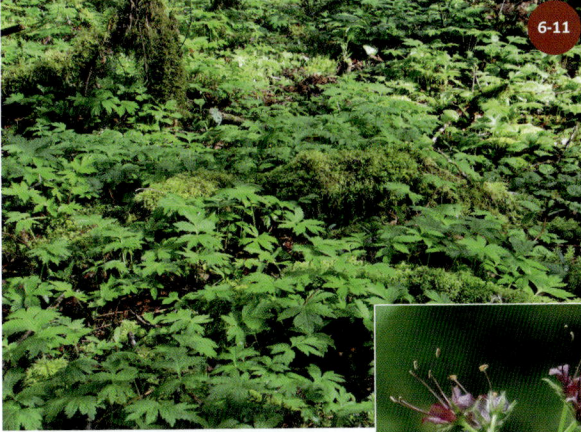

6-11 *Hydrophyllum tenuipes* (Pacific waterleaf) occurs only in the southern part of our region. A member of the waterleaf family, its flowers are conspicuous for their long stamens rather than for their dull purple petals (inset).

6-12 *Pectiantia ovalis* (oval-leaved mitrewort) is the only one of BC's six mitrewort species expected in the dry belt lowlands. All other species are either of higher elevations, wetter climates or different distribution geographically. The intricate floral pattern in *Pectiantia*, with branched petals, is a further example of flower diversity in the saxifrage family (compare 6-8 *Tolmiea*). Another distinctive feature in *Pectiantia* is that the seeds are dislodged or dispersed by rain hitting the up-facing cups in which they are ripening (Brodie, 1951).

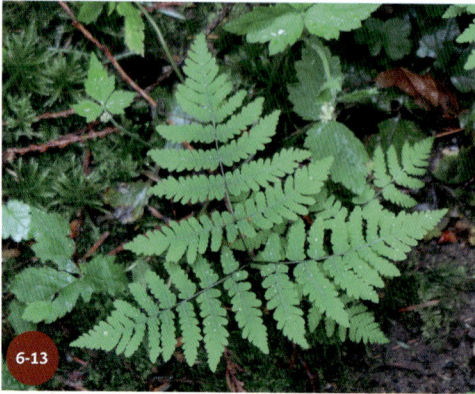

6-13

6-13 *Gymnocarpium disjunctum* (western oak fern) is a sporadic component of this forest but is common further west and at higher elevation. Oak ferns are composed of two different species, ours and *Gymnocarpium dryopteris*. Using image 6-13, move up one rung from the main junction of the three triangular parts of the plant. If the opposing pinnules closest to this branching point are unequal in length, you have *G. disjunctum*. If they are near equal, you have *G. dryopteris*.

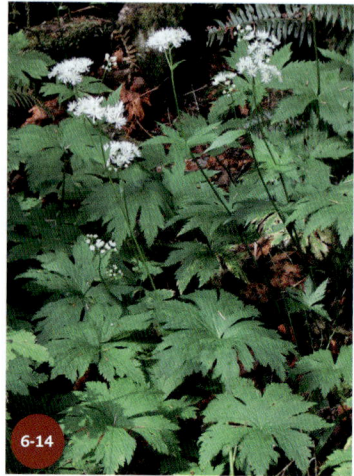

6-14

6-14 *Trautvetteria caroliniensis* (false bugbane) is another tall member of the buttercup family without petals. But the flowers are showy due to the large white stamens.

6-15 *Viola glabella* (stream violet) is one of our three yellow-flowered violets and is also common along smaller water courses.

6-15

6-16

Finally, the only common moss that we have not yet encountered is **6-16 *Rhytidiadelphus loreus* (lanky moss)**. On average it is smaller than 1-33 *Rhytidiadelphus triquetrus* (goose-necked moss) and has more even-leaved slender shoots. It is also a dominant ground cover in coastal forests with moister climates.

Garry Oak Plant Communities

How do you recognize these communities?

Garry oak (**7-1** *Quercus garryana*) is the only or the most frequent tree in these communities, but Douglas-fir and, rarely, arbutus may occur as scattered individuals. Shrub layers may be absent, dominated by common snowberry or by oceanspray. Species-rich and seasonally colourful herb and grass layers are often present.

Despite occupying such a small portion of the coastal dry belt, Garry oak plant communities hold the largest assemblage of attractive native plants. For colourful wildflowers, it is hard to beat the Garry oak ecosystem.

We present Garry oak vegetation in two parts: Garry Oak Parklands and Garry Oak Woodlands. In today's context, the plural in Parklands is something of an exaggeration—a bio-regional "remembrance of things past"—because very few examples of them are left after some 180 years of occupation, agricultural activities and urbanization by non-Indigenous people.

7-1 *Quercus garryana* (**Garry oak**) in a parkland setting.

The parkland and woodland settings are distinguished by the following features:

Garry Oak Parklands	Garry Oak Woodlands
· openings in the tree and shrub cover	· more even tree and shrub cover
· gentle or flat topography	· more rugged topography
· deeper soils	· shallower soils or mosaic of soil and rock

The present popular term "Garry oak meadows" is roughly equivalent ecologically to our Garry oak parklands.

7a Garry Oak Parkland

The nearly two centuries of occupation by non-Indigenous people has also led to an influx of non-native plants, even in plant communities where the soil has not been physically altered. More than elsewhere, this is the case for the Garry oak parklands. One of the reasons is that for many decades they were the preferred and most accessible areas for domestic grazing.

Many of these meadows now have a complete lack of once dominant native grasses, such as California oatgrass, junegrass, Sandberg's bluegrass, Roemer's fescue and Pacific fescue. These have all been replaced by weedy introduced grasses and other non-native herbs.

7-3

7-3

7-4

7-4 *Bromus carinatus* (California brome) is a tall (to 80 cm) grass that is a characteristic species of all Garry oak communities.

7-3 Camassia quamash (common camas) closeup.

2-13

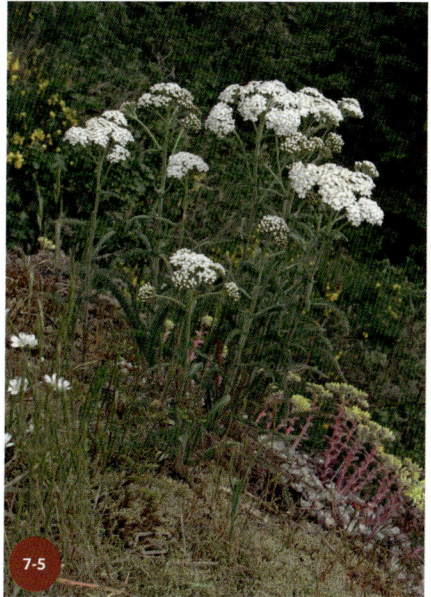

7-5

First introduced to us in section 2, 2-13 *Elymus glaucus* (blue wildrye) is always recognized by its straight stems and flowering spikes.

7-5 *Achillea millefolium* (yarrow) is found in open, sunny habitats, including meadows, rock outcrops and in woodland openings.

Table 7a: Garry Oak Parkland

Shrub Layer	%
Symphoricarpos albus (common snowberry)	32

Moss Layer	%
Niphotrichum elongatum (elongate racomitrium moss)	27

Herb Layer	%
Bromus carinatus (California brome)	86
Cerastium arvense (field chickweed)	86
Achillea millefolium (yarrow)	82
Elymus glaucus (blue wildrye)	82
Sanicula crassicaulis (Pacific sanicle)	82
Camassia leichtlinii (great camas)	73
Claytonia perfoliata (miner's-lettuce)	68
Collinsia parviflora (small-flowered blue-eyed Mary)	50
Ranunculus occidentalis (western buttercup)	50
Triteleia hyacinthina (white triteleia)	50
Delphinium menziesii (Menzies' larkspur)	36
Lomatium utriculatum (spring gold)	36
Nemophila parviflora (small-flowered nemophila)	36
Camassia quamash (common camas)	32
Fritillaria affinis (chocolate lily)	32
Carex inops (long-stoloned sedge)	27
Olsynium douglasii (satinflower)	27

Herb Layer	%
Polypodium glycyrrhiza (licorice fern)	27
Lupinus bicolor (two-coloured lupine)	27
Trifolium microcephalum (small-headed clover)	23
Allium acuminatum (Hooker's onion)	18
Primula hendersonii (broad-leaved shootingstar)	18
Lomatium nudicaule (barestem desert-parsley)	18
Acmispon parviflorus (small-flowered birds-foot trefoil)	18
Melica subulata (Alaska oniongrass)	18
Pentagramma triangularis (goldenback fern)	18
Trifolium oliganthum (few-flowered clover)	18
Trifolium willldenovii (tomcat clover)	18
Lithophragma parviflorum (small-flowered fringecup)	14
Micranthes integrifolia (meadow saxifrage)	14
Brodiaea coronaria (harvest brodiaea)	14

Tree Layer	%
Quercus garryana (Garry oak)	100

> 75% chance of seeing this species
50–75% chance of seeing this species
25–49% chance of seeing this species
< 25% chance of seeing this species

Non-native	%
Galium aparine (cleavers)	100
Vicia sativa (common vetch)	100
Cytisus scoparius (Scotch broom)	95
Geranium molle (dovefoot geranium)	86
Bromus sterilis (barren brome)	82
Poa pratensis (Kentucky bluegrass)	77
Vulpia bromoides (barren fescue)	77
Vicia hirsuta (tiny vetch)	68
Cynosurus echinatus (hedgehog dogtail)	59
Stellaria media (common chickweed)	55
Bromus hordeaceus (soft brome)	50
Bromus diandrus ssp. *rigidus* (rip-gut brome)	41

Non-native	%
Aira praecox (early hairgrass)	36
Rumex acetosella (sheep sorrel)	32
Hypochaeris radicata (hairy cat's-ear)	27
Turritis glabra (tower mustard)	27
Dactylis glomerata (orchard grass)	23
Aira caryophyllea (silver hairgrass)	18
Plantago lanceolata (ribwort plantain)	18
Veronica arvensis (wall speedwell)	18
Festuca rubra (red fescue)	10
Holcus lanatus (common velvet-grass)	10
Bromus tectorum (cheatgrass)	5
Myosotis discolor (common forget-me-not)	5

The prevalence of introduced species is made obvious in Table 7a, where introduced species have been listed with their frequency of occurrence. Note how **7-2 *Camassia leichtlinii* (great camas)** and **7-3 *Camassia quamash* (common camas)** are listed below several non-native species in terms of frequency. However, it is the camas species that are the most conspicuous and often produce the most biomass. *Camassia leichtlinii* (great camas) has large bulbs and grows taller than *Camassia quamash* (common camas), but common camas usually grows in dense stands that form bright blue patches on shallow soils, as shown on pages 69–70.

When in bloom, the two species are easily distinguished by their flower symmetry and by the fashion in which the flower parts wilt after blooming. *Camassia quamash* has slightly bilaterally symmetric flowers, and its tepals curl up individually when they wilt, while *Camassia leichtlinii* has a radially symmetric flower with petals that twist together into a single tube upon wilting.

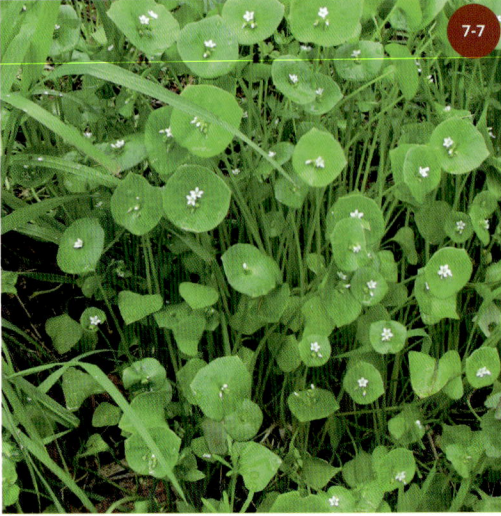

7-7 Claytonia perfoliata (miner's-lettuce) has a flowering stem that appears to grow through the top leaf. Despite the specific name *perfoliata*, which translates as "through the leaf," it is actually two leaves that have wrapped around the stem and have merged into a round disc. This species is distinguished from 23-15 *Claytonia parviflora* (streambank springbeauty) by having broadly diamond-shaped basal leaf blades rather than linear ones.

Also first introduced in section 2, 2-7 *Sanicula crassicaulis* (Pacific sanicle) is common in dry forests, woodlands and meadows.

7-6 Cerastium arvense (field chickweed), despite its common name, is not a weed but a native plant of open habitats.

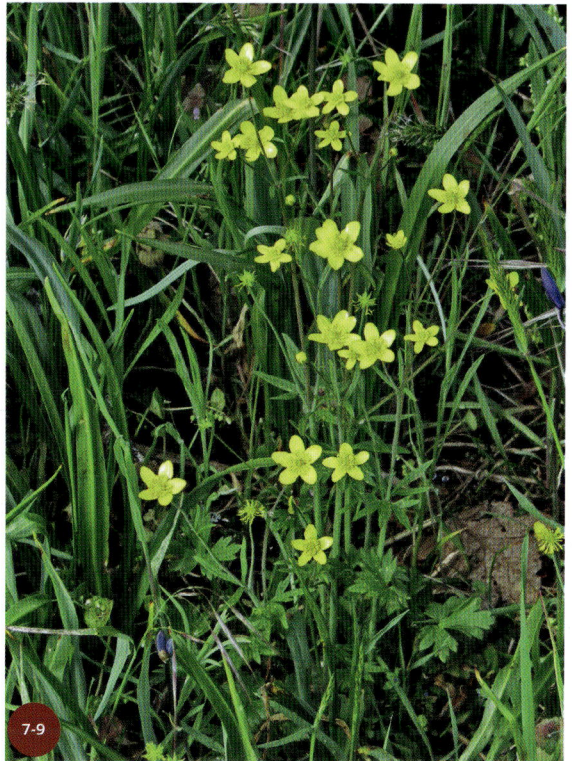

7-8 *Delphinium menziesii* **(Menzies' larkspur)** belongs to the buttercup family and grows from a small black tuber that helps it survive the summer drought. **7-9** *Ranunculus occidentalis* **(western buttercup)** is in the same family as *Delphinium menziesii*, but only the basal leaves indicate this relationship.

Underground storage systems of several kinds, including bulbs, corms, thickened roots and tubers, are a characteristic in many meadow plants associated with Garry oak. They are found in the two camas species, in chocolate lilies, onions, white triteleia, harvest brodiaeas, shootingstars, common yampah root, orchids, fawn lilies and species of *Lomatium*. Collectively, plants equipped with such storage organs are called geophytes.

7-10

Along with camas bulbs, the bulbs of **7-10** *Fritillaria affinis* **(chocolate lily)** were eaten by Indigenous peoples. However, chocolate lilies do not occur in vast quantities like camas does.

7-11

7-11 *Triteleia hyacinthina* **(white triteleia)** flowers in early summer when the many non-native annual grasses are starting to dry up. White triteleia, also known as "fool's onions," has the general appearance of onions but is easily distinguished by not having the characteristic onion smell when crushed. The hollow leaves of immature white triteleia plants occur by the thousands, especially in seepage sites, and only a tiny fraction of them ever come to bloom.

7-13 *Olsynium douglasii* **(satinflower)**, **7-12** *Lomatium utriculatum* **(spring gold)**, **7-35** *Plectritis congesta* **(sea blush, p. 87)**, and **7-14** *Collinsia parviflora* **(small-flowered blue-eyed Mary)** are among the best known and earliest blooming wildflowers. *Collinsia parviflora* often flowers together with the contrasting yellow of *Lomatium utriculatum*. The dense carpet of **7-30** *Niphotrichum elongatum* **(elongate racomitrium moss)** makes the spring gold stand out in the top left photo but is more typical for the hill-country pocket grasslands of section 9a, where it is even more common.

7-15 *Carex inops* **(long-stoloned sedge)** is an important component of Garry oak communities, both under trees and in open areas. It can form large colonies. There is no other narrow-leaved sedge in this environment with which to confuse it.

7-16 *Primula hendersonii* (broad-leaved shootingstar), formerly known as *Dodecatheon hendersonii*, a graceful springtime bloomer, is equally common in the Garry oak woodlands (section 7b), as well as in shore pine–Douglas-fir–arbutus woodlands (section 8).

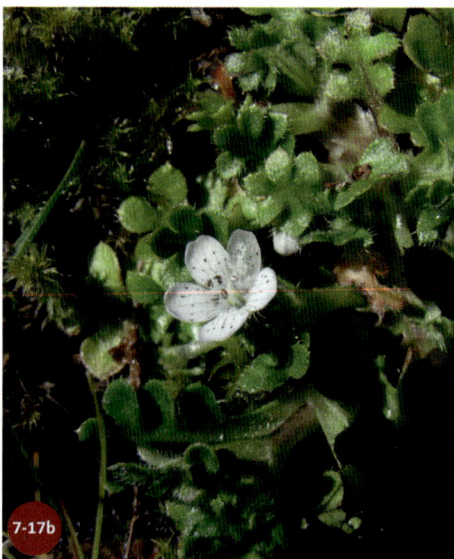

7-17a *Nemophila parviflora* (small-flowered nemophila) is a member of the *Hydrophyllaceae* (waterleaf family). It has elongated trailing shoots, as opposed to its even smaller cousin, **7-17b *Nemophila pedunculata* (meadow nemophila)**, which forms tight clumps. Key features are tiny appendages to the calyx, not visible in our images.

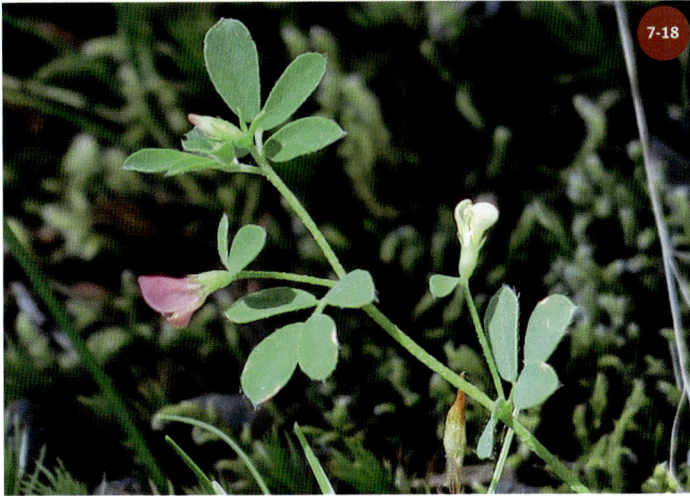

7-18 *Acmispon parviflorus* (small-flowered birds-foot trefoil), formerly *Lotus micranthus*, is a tiny legume with red and yellow in its flowers, which later form minute "pea pods."

In the same family (*Fabaceae*) is **7-19 *Trifolium microcephalum* (small-headed clover)**. Small-headed clover is very similar to **7-20 *Trifolium microdon* (thimble clover)**. Hand lens examination reveals that the calyx of the tiny flower is hairy in the former and hairless in the latter.

7-21

7-21

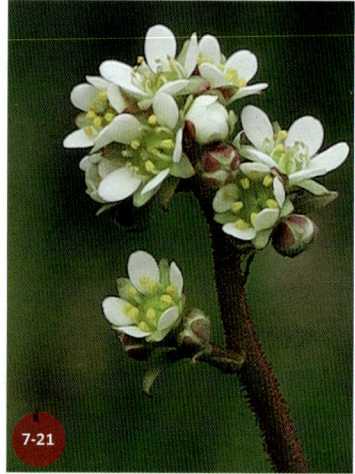

7-22

Saxifrages—literally "rock breakers" in Latin— are usually thought of as high-elevation plants, or at least as rock dwellers, but **7-21 *Micranthes integrifolia* (meadow saxifrage)** is neither. It is a meadow or grassland plant, quite happy at sea level. The generic name in **7-22 *Lithophragma parviflorum* (small-flowered fringecup)** also refers to rock (Greek *lithos*), with the *-phragma* meaning a partition or fence. So, here too, rock breaker is close to its meaning. In Garry oak communities, small-flowered fringecup rarely grows on bare rock, unlike its smaller cousin, smooth fringecup.

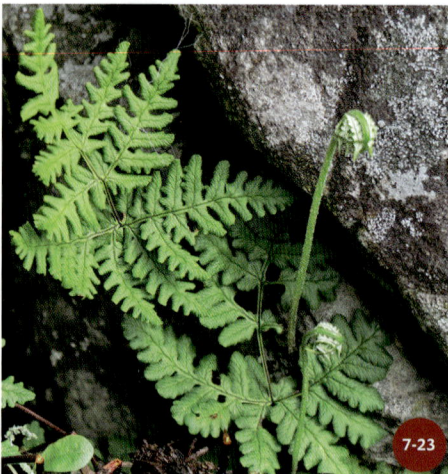

7-23

7-23 *Pentagramma triangularis* is the striking **goldenback fern**. In our image the telltale powdery-white underside is only visible on the unrolling young shoots but would stand out if the mature fronds were turned upside-down.

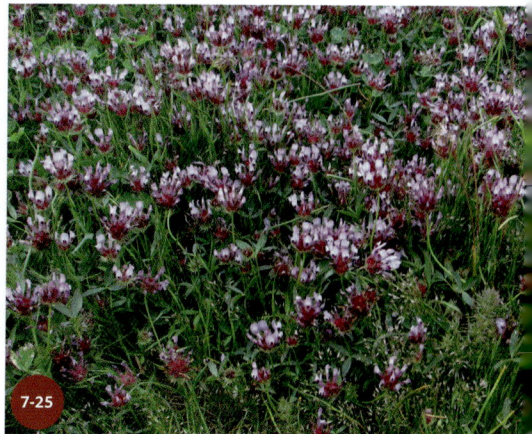

7-24 *Trifolium oliganthum* (few-flowered clover) is like a miniature version of the more robust **7-25 *Trifolium willdenovii* (tomcat clover).** Both are annuals, arising from seed every year, which means there may be few of them one year and large patches of them another.

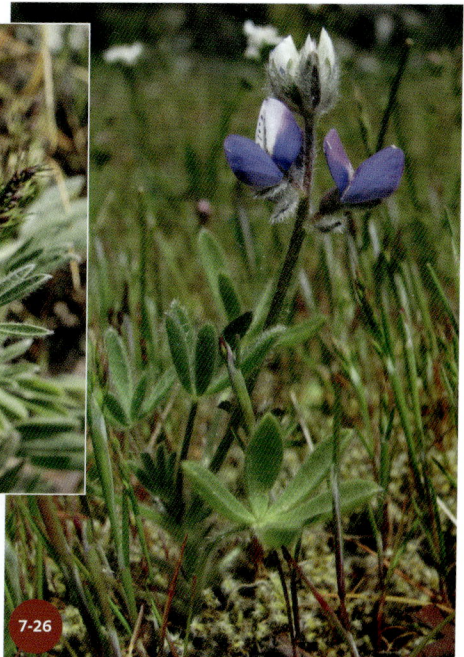

Like *T. oliganthum* and *willdenovii*, **7-26 *Lupinus bicolor* (two-coloured lupine)** is another member of the *Leguminosae* family. It too is an annual from seed and can vary in number from year to year. Closer examination of the flowers of this dwarf lupine reveals that there are actually three colours: white, blue and pink.

7-27 *Lomatium nudicaule* **(barestem desert-parsley)** grows from massive, starchy roots. Some Indigenous peoples ate the young leaves as a springtime green, but it is mostly the seeds that remain culturally important as medicine for colds and coughs. The plant is also used as an incense for spiritual purposes (N. Turner, p.c., 2023).

7-28 *Allium acuminatum* **(Hooker's onion)** is the common onion in dry meadows.

7-29 *Brodiaea coronaria* **(harvest brodiaea)** flowers when other plants wither away for their summer rest.

7b Garry Oak Woodland

Most species listed and pictured in 7a Garry Oak Parkland are also present here, albeit with different frequencies. Many species familiar to us from the forest communities of well-drained sites also occur in this woodland setting, making Garry Oak Woodland by far the most diverse plant community portrayed in this guide.

The main floristic distinctions of this community are an increased number of shrubs and the presence of 2-8 *Erythronium oregonum* (white fawn lily) in all sampled stands. As well, the greater presence of 2-14 *Polypodium glycyrrhiza* (licorice fern) indicates this woodland community includes portions of shallow soil over bedrock. The moss/lichen layer is also much richer in species than in the parkland setting.

Images following the Garry Oak Woodland table are of species not pictured so far in this guide, not necessarily of those most conspicuous in this community.

Introduced species are only somewhat less common in this setting than in the Garry oak parkland setting, with *Geranium molle* (dovefoot geranium) and *Poa pratensis* (Kentucky bluegrass) less frequent, and some weedy plants absent, but with other weeds, such as *Anthoxantum odoratum* (sweet vernalgrass) more dominant.

Quercus garryana (Garry oak) woodland featuring *Erythronium oregonum* (white fawn lily).

Table 7b: Garry Oak Woodland

Tree Layer	%
Quercus garryana (Garry oak)	100
Pseudotsuga menziesii (Douglas-fir)	26
Arbutus menziesii (arbutus)	17

Shrub Layer	%
Symphoricarpos albus (common snowberry)	96
Holodiscus discolor (oceanspray)	91
Mahonia aquifolium (tall Oregon-grape)	78
Rosa gymnocarpa (baldhip rose)	39
Amelanchier alnifolia (saskatoon)	26
Lonicera ciliosa (orange honeysuckle)	22
Rubus ursinus (trailing blackberry)	17
Lonicera hispidula (hairy honeysuckle)	13

Moss/Lichen Layer	%
Rhytidiadelphus triquetrus (goose-necked moss)	70
Dicranum scoparium (broom moss)	61
Niphotrichum elongatum (elongate racomitrium moss)	35
Kindbergia oregana (Oregon beaked-moss)	30
Polytrichum juniperinum (juniper haircap moss)	30
Hylocomium splendens (step moss)	17
Antitrichia californica (Californian hanging moss)	17
Cladonia furcata (forked cladonia)	17

> 75% chance of seeing this species
50–75% chance of seeing this species
25–49% chance of seeing this species
< 25% chance of seeing this species

Quercus garryana (Garry oak) woodland.

Herb Layer	%
Erythronium oregonum (white fawn lily)	100
Elymus glaucus (blue wildrye)	96
Polypodium glycyrrhiza (licorice fern)	96
Camassia leichtlinii (great camas)	91
Melica subulata (Alaska oniongrass)	87
Sanicula crassicaulis (Pacific sanicle)	83
Lathyrus nevadensis (purple peavine)	74
Montia parvifolia (small-leaved montia)	74
Carex inops (long-stoloned sedge)	70
Heuchera micrantha (small-flowered alumroot)	70
Luzula comosa var. laxa (Pacific woodrush)	70
Moehringia macrophylla (big-leaved sandwort)	70
Sedum spathulifolium (broad-leaved stonecrop)	70
Plectritis congesta (sea blush)	65
Achillea millefolium (yarrow)	61
Delphinium menziesii (Menzies' larkspur)	61
Primula hendersonii (broad-leaved shootingstar)	61
Bromus carinatus (California brome)	57
Cerastium arvense (field chickweed)	52
Polystichum munitum (sword fern)	52
Camassia quamash (common camas)	49
Ranunculus occidentalis (western buttercup)	49
Festuca occidentalis (western fescue)	43
Selaginella wallacei (Wallace's selaginella)	43
Toxicoscordion venenosum (death camas)	43
Triteleia hyacinthina (white triteleia)	43
Claytonia perfoliata (miner's-lettuce)	39
Fritillaria affinis (chocolate lily)	39
Acmispon parviflorus (small-flowered birds-foot trefoil)	35
Danthonia californica (California oatgrass)	35
Fragaria virginiana (wild strawberry)	35

Herb Layer	%
Olsynium douglasii (satinflower)	35
Trifolium oliganthum (few-flowered clover)	35
Vicia americana (American vetch)	35
Cardamine oligosperma (little western bittercress)	30
Collinsia parviflora (small-flowered blue-eyed Mary)	30
Festuca roemeri (Roemer's fescue)	26
Lysimachia latifolia (broad-leaved starflower)	26
Micranthes integrifolia (meadow saxifrage)	26
Nemophila parviflora (small-flowered nemophila)	26
Platanthera elegans (elegant rein orchid)	26
Arctostaphylos uva-ursi (kinnikinnick)	22
Lomatium nudicaule (barestem desert-parsley)	22
Lomatium utriculatum (spring gold)	22
Sanicula graveolens (Sierra sanicle)	22
Trifolium microdon (thimble clover)	22
Clinopodium douglasii (yerba buena)	17
Erythranthe alsinoides (chickweed monkeyflower)	17
Osmorhiza berteroi (mountain sweet-cicely)	17
Trifolium microcephalum (small-headed clover)	17
Trifolium willdenovii (tomcat clover)	17
Allium acuminatum (Hooker's onion)	13
Eriophyllum lanatum (woolly sunflower)	13
Fragaria vesca (wood strawberry)	13
Goodyera oblongifolia (rattlesnake plantain)	13
Hieracium albiflorum (white hawkweed)	13
Perideridia montana (common yampah)	13
Plectritis macrocera (long-spurred plectritis)	13

7-31 *Sedum spathulifolium* (broad-leaved stonecrop) is equally common under a tree canopy and in open sites. Prolific flowering occurs only in the latter.

7-32 *Montia parvifolia* (small-leaved montia) grows in moss carpets and on thin soil layers over rock, usually in part shade or on north-facing slopes. It is also known as spider plant on account of its thin runners that spread in all directions.

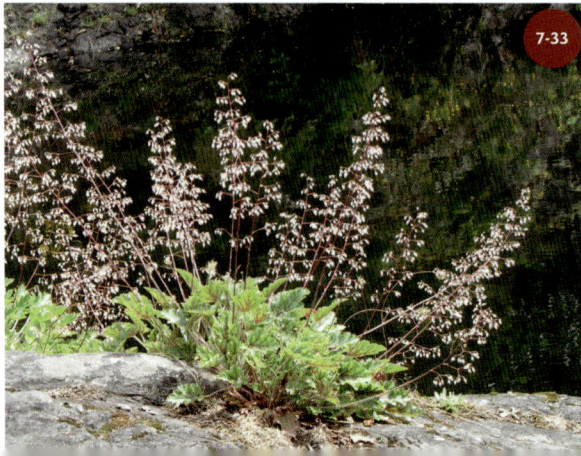

7-33 *Heuchera micrantha* (small-flowered alumroot) often roots in crevices of the rock, both in sunny and part-shady habitats.

7-34 *Luzula comosa* var. *laxa* (Pacific woodrush) is one of the woodrushes that were collectively called *Luzula multiflora* until recently. It prefers open grassy habitats.

7-35 *Plectritis congesta* (sea blush) is a common and attractive annual of shallow soils and mossy rock outcrops. Our image shows it with the smaller pale-flowered **7-36 *Plectritis macrocera* (long-spurred plectritis)**. However, they are not often found together.

7-37 *Selaginella wallacei* (Wallace's selaginella) is a small spore-bearing plant related to clubmosses and may be mistaken for a moss. It occurs in almost half of all shallow-soil Garry oak sites.

7-38 *Fragaria virginiana* (wild strawberry) is often called blueleaf strawberry to distinguish it from 2-16 *Fragaria vesca* (wood strawberry). *F. virginiana* can be found with similar frequency in the shore pine–Douglas-fir–arbutus woodlands habitat (section 8 in this guide).

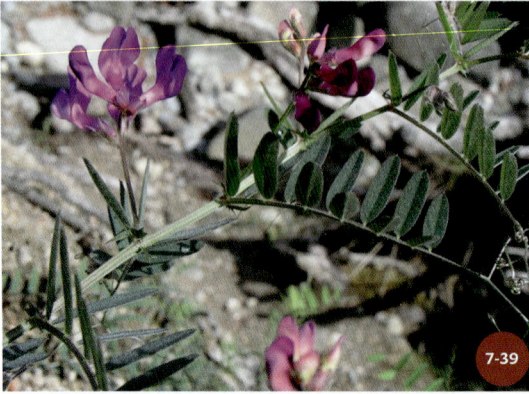

7-39 Vicia americana (American vetch) is the only native vetch in the Garry oak communities. The other vetches, even more common in the Garry oak realm, are all introduced weeds.

If you smell a strong cilantro-like odour while walking through a Garry oak woodland, you have probably stepped on **7-40 Sanicula graveolens (Sierra sanicle)**. The species name *graveolens* translates as "heavily scented." Sierra sanicle is distinguished from the more common 2-7 Pacific sanicle by its deeply divided leaves and less robust stature.

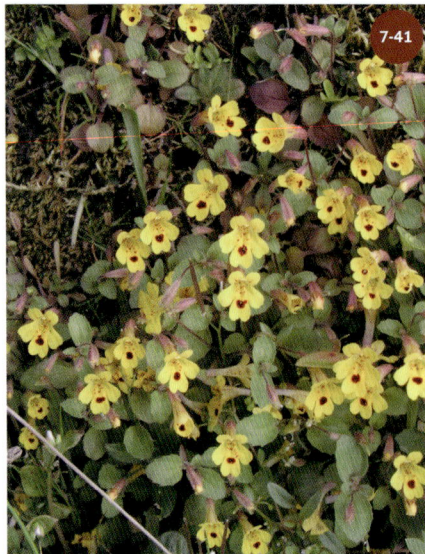

7-41 Erythranthe alsinoides (chickweed monkeyflower) is one of the first plants to flower locally, usually in February and March. It grows in rock crevices, under rock overhangs and in moss carpets. Only the moss carpet micro-habitat counts toward its 17 percent frequency in Table 7b.

9-3 *Festuca roemeri* (Roemer's fescue) and 9-18 *Perideridia montana* (common yampah) are considerably more frequent in the hill-country pocket grasslands of section 9 and will be described there. In 1970 Roemer's fescue was discovered locally by the senior author of this guide and has since been found to occur all the way south to California.

In addition to 7-30 *Niphotrichum elongatum*, there are three species in the moss/lichen layer we have met before. They are all species of forests and woodlands: 1-33 *Rhytidiadelphus triquetrus* (goose-necked moss), 1-32 *Kindbergia oregana* (Oregon beaked-moss) and 1-34 *Hylocomium splendens* (step moss).

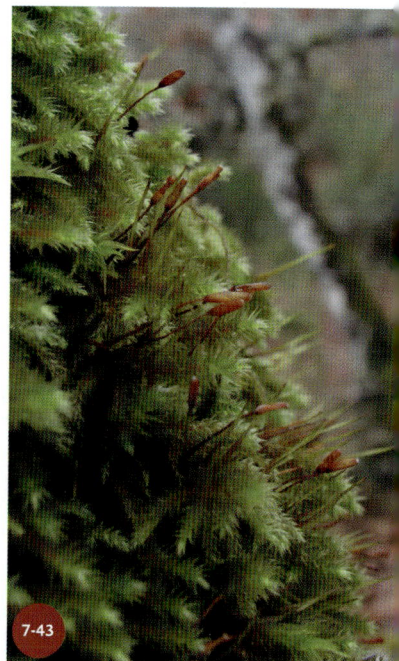

These are augmented by two additional species: a lichen, **7-42 *Cladonia furcata* (forked cladonia)**, and a moss, **7-43 *Antitrichia californica* (Californian hanging moss)**. Microscopic features are needed to distinguish the latter from *Isothecium cristatum* (isothecium moss) and *Antitrichia curtipendula* (pendulous wing-moss).

Two more species, 8-5 *Dicranum scoparium* (broom moss) and 8-6 *Polytrichum juniperinum* (juniper haircap moss) are shared with the shore pine–Douglas-fir–arbutus woodlands habitat. They are featured in section 8.

8 Shore Pine–Douglas-fir–Arbutus Woodland

How do you recognize this woodland?

The combination of shore pine and hairy manzanita pinpoints this woodland. The presence of Douglas-firs and arbutus is variable.

On hill tops and south-facing slopes between 250 and 450 metre elevation, this woodland is the connecting link between open rocky terrain, grass balds (the pocket grasslands of section 9) and closed conifer forests. In this elevation band, the conifer forests themselves, especially those on flat or gently sloping ground, are outside of the coastal dry belt. However, on dry, open rocky terrain and south-facing slopes, the species combination has strong affinities with the lowland Douglas-fir–arbutus forest and Garry oak communities (see sections 2 and 7).

8-1 *Pinus contorta* var. *contorta* (shore pine) is the only new tree found here. Other tree species common in this woodland are known to us from the Douglas-fir forest and the Douglas-fir–arbutus forest: Douglas-fir (1-1), arbutus (2-1) and Scouler's willow (2-2).

Table 8: Shore Pine-Douglas-fir-Arbutus Woodland

Tree Layer	%
Pinus contorta var. *contorta* (shore pine)	100
Pseudotsuga menziesii (Douglas-fir)	87
Arbutus menziesii (arbutus)	83
Salix scouleriana (Scouler's willow)	23

Shrub Layer	%
Arctostaphylos columbiana (hairy manzanita)	93
Holodiscus discolor (oceanspray)	83
Rosa gymnocarpa (baldhip rose)	83
Gaultheria shallon (salal)	67
Paxistima myrsinites (falsebox)	67
Mahonia aquifolium (tall Oregon-grape)	60
Mahonia nervosa (dull Oregon-grape)	57
Symphoricarpos hesperius (trailing snowberry)	47
Amelanchier alnifolia (saskatoon)	23
Lonicera hispidula (hairy honeysuckle)	20

Moss Layer	%
Kindbergia oregana (Oregon beaked-moss)	97
Dicranum scoparium (broom moss)	80
Rhytidiadelphus triquetrus (goose-necked moss)	73
Polytrichum juniperinum (juniper haircap moss)	57
Homalothecium megaptilum (trachybryum moss)	20

Herb Layer	%
Elymus glaucus (blue wildrye)	87
Platanthera transversa (royal rein orchid)	80
Festuca occidentalis (western fescue)	70
Festuca rubra (red fescue, a native subspecies)	67
Goodyera oblongifolia (rattlesnake plantain)	67
Hieracium albiflorum (white hawkweed)	67
Lysimachia latifolia (broad-leaved starflower)	60
Sanicula crassicaulis (Pacific sanicle)	57
Bromus vulgaris (Columbia brome)	50
Danthonia californica (California oatgrass)	47
Melica subulata (Alaska oniongrass)	47
Fragaria virginiana (wild strawberry)	37
Primula hendersonii (broad-leaved shootingstar)	33
Trisetum canescens (tall trisetum)	30
Triteleia hyacinthina (white triteleia)	30
Achillea millefolium (yarrow)	27
Arctostaphylos uva-ursi (kinnikinnick)	27
Toxicoscordion venenosum (death camas)	27
Calypso bulbosa (fairy slipper)	20
Camassia quamash (common camas)	20
Carex inops (long-stoloned sedge)	20
Erythronium oregonum (white fawn lily)	20
Lilium columbianum (tiger lily)	20

Non-native

Cytisus scoparius (Scotch broom)

Anthoxanthum odoratum (sweet vernalgrass)

Hypochaeris radicata (hairy cat's-ear)

Galium aparine (cleavers)

> 75% chance of seeing this species
50–75% chance of seeing this species
25–49% chance of seeing this species
< 25% chance of seeing this species

Of the many shrubs encountered in this woodland, only one, **8-2 *Arctostaphylos columbiana*** (**hairy manzanita**), is new. This is an attractive evergreen shrub with smooth, brown bark reminiscent of the related arbutus. The name manzanita means "little apple" in Spanish— a perfect name to describe the tiny apple-like fruit this shrub bears later in the summer.

Other shrubs are those also found in the Douglas-fir and the Douglas-fir–arbutus forests. Shrubs occurring in more than half of the sampled woodlands are, in order of decreasing frequency, 1-13 *Holodiscus discolor* (oceanspray), 1-11 *Rosa gymnocarpa* (baldhip rose), 1-10 *Gaultheria shallon* (salal), 2-5 *Paxistima myrsinites* (falsebox), 2-4 *Mahonia aquifolium* (tall Oregon-grape) and 1-8 *Mahonia nervosa* (dull Oregon-grape). Less frequent shrubs are 1-17 *Symphoricarpos hesperius* (trailing snowberry), 1-18 *Amelanchier alnifolia* (saskatoon) and 2-3 *Lonicera hispidula* (hairy honeysuckle).

In the herb layer of this community, all species, with the exception of **8-3 *Festuca rubra* (red fescue)**, that attain 50 or more percent frequency have already been encountered in the Douglas-fir and Douglas-fir–arbutus forests.

The ninth species sometimes found in Garry oak communities but mainly found in this habitat is **8-4 *Arctostaphylos uva-ursi* (kinnikinnick)**. An evergreen woody shrub with leathery dark green leaves, it can be found growing close to the ground. *Arctostaphylos uva-ursi* and *Arctostaphylos columbiana* can hybridize. The result, ***Arctostaphylos × media* (northwestern manzanita)**, has leaves a bit larger than kinnikinnick that are often covered with very fine downy hair.

There are another nine species with less than 50 percent frequency that are all characteristic members of Garry oak communities and/or open grasslands (sections 7 and 9). We have been introduced to six of them in Garry oak communities: 7-38 *Fragaria virginiana* (wild strawberry), 7-16 *Primula hendersonii* (broad-leaved shooting-star), 7-11 *Triteleia hyacinthina* (white triteleia), 7-5 *Achillea millefolium* (yarrow), 7-3 *Camassia quamash* (common camas) and 7-15 *Carex inops* (long-stoloned sedge). Two of the species, 9-2 *Danthonia californica* (California oatgrass) and 9-5 *Toxicoscordion venenosum* (death camas), will be discussed in the hill-country pocket grasslands habitat (section 9), where they appear with greater frequency.

8-5 *Dicranum scoparium* (broom moss) and **8-6 *Polytrichum juniperinum* (juniper haircap moss)** can also be found in Garry oak woodlands, but they occur with much higher frequency in this habitat. **8-7 *Homalothecium megaptilum* (trachybryum moss)** is introduced here for the first time.

Two of the mosses in the shore pine–Douglas-fir–arbutus woodland are familiar to us from the Douglas-fir forests: 1-32 *Kindbergia oregana* (Oregon beaked-moss) and 1-33 *Rhytidiadelphus triquetrus* (goose-necked moss).

Hill-country Pocket Grassland Communities

How do you recognize these grasslands?

Natural grassy openings at elevations near the upper limit or above the occurrence of Garry oaks fit this description. They are usually associated with shallow soils and can be under the influence of seepage.

Whereas Garry oak woodlands and savannahs generally occupy lowlands up to 200 metres above sea level, a vegetation type with strong floristic relationships to them occurs under special conditions on south-facing slopes between 250 and 450 metres. The combination of southern aspect, shallow soils, and relatively warm and dry microclimates results in grassland openings surrounded by evergreen forest. The surrounding trees are Douglas-firs, shore pines and arbutus. Garry oak is largely absent in these grassland openings and their surroundings. Seasonal seepage sites containing some of the more interesting plant combinations also occur in these grasslands.

Pocket grasslands.

Seasonal seepage sites in pocket grasslands.

Many species of the "Garry oak herb layer" reappear in these openings, combined with native grasses. These grasslands are of particular significance, not only because they represent pockets of rare plant diversity, but also because they can give us clues as to the original species combination of the now greatly altered herb and grass layers in the lower-elevation Garry oak communities.

9a Hill-country Pocket Grasslands

Table 9a: Hill-country Pocket Grasslands

Herb Layer	%
Danthonia californica (California oatgrass)	90
Camassia quamash (common camas)	72
Acmispon parviflorus (small-flowered birds-foot trefoil)	66
Eriophyllum lanatum (woolly sunflower)	64
Achillea millefolium (yarrow)	63
Festuca roemeri (Roemer's fescue)	60
Lomatium utriculatum (spring gold)	59
Triteleia hyacinthina (white triteleia)	57

Herb Layer	%
Toxicoscordion venenosum (death camas)	55
Carex inops (long-stoloned sedge)	54
Brodiaea coronaria (harvest brodiaea)	52
Trifolium willdenovii (tomcat clover)	50
Cerastium arvense (field chickweed)	46
Trifolium microcephalum (small-headed clover)	46
Luzula comosa var. *laxa* (Pacific woodrush)	45

Herb Layer	%
Madia gracilis (slender tarweed)	39
Leptosiphon minimus (bicoloured linanthus)	37
Koeleria macrantha (junegrass)	34
Plectritis congesta (sea blush)	30
Allium acuminatum (Hooker's onion)	29
Ranunculus occidentalis (western buttercup)	29
Daucus pusillus (wild carrot)	27
Delphinium menziesii (Menzies' larkspur)	27
Elymus glaucus (blue wildrye)	26
Clarkia amoena (farewell-to-spring)	25
Microsteris gracilis (slender phlox)	25
Trifolium microdon (thimble clover)	25
Triphysaria pusilla (dwarf owl-clover)	25
Achnatherum lemmonii (Lemmon's needlegrass)	24

Moss Layer	%
Niphotrichum elongatum (elongate racomitrium moss)	81
Homalothecium aeneum (golden curly moss)	49
Polytrichum juniperinum (juniper haircap moss)	29
Syntrichia ruralis (hair screw-moss)	28
Dicranum scoparium (broom moss)	16

> 75% chance of seeing this species
50–75% chance of seeing this species
25–49% chance of seeing this species
< 25% chance of seeing this species

Herb Layer	%
Trifolium oliganthum (few-flowered clover)	20
Primula hendersonii (broad-leaved shootingstar)	20
Primula pauciflora var. *pauciflora* (pretty shootingstar)	20
Collinsia parviflora (small-flowered blue-eyed Mary)	17
Agrostis pallens (dune bentgrass)	16
Agoseris grandiflora (large-flowered agoseris)	16
Perideridia montana (common yampah)	16
Prunella vulgaris (self-heal)	14
Castilleja attenuata (narrow-leaved paintbrush)	13
Agoseris heterophylla (annual agoseris)	13

Non-native

Aira caryophyllea (silver hairgrass)
Bromus hordeaceus (soft brome)
Hypochaeris radicata (hairy cat's-ear)
Veronica arvensis (wall speedwell)
Vulpia bromoides (barren fescue)
Aira praecox (early hairgrass)
Cynosurus echinatus (hedgehog dogtail)
Hypochaeris glabra (smooth cat's-ear)
Silene gallica (common catchfly)
Anthoxanthum odoratum (sweet vernalgrass)
Myosotis discolor (common forget-me-not)
Rumex acetosella (sheep sorrel)
Cytisus scoparius (Scotch broom)
Silene antirrhina (sleepy catchfly)
Bromus sterilis (barren brome)
Galium aparine (cleavers)
Hypericum perforatum (St. John's-wort)
Trifolium dubium (small hop-clover)

With the exception of **9-1 *Eriophyllum lanatum* (woolly sunflower)**, we have already encountered all of the 12 species occurring with 50 percent or higher frequency in Table 9a in the Garry oak communities (sections 7a and 7b).

This image shows the edge of a grassland opening with **9-1 *Eriophyllum lanatum* (woolly sunflower)**, 7-5 *Achillea millefolium* (yarrow) and **9-3 *Festuca roemeri* (Roemer's fescue)**, all in a carpet of 7-30 *Niphotrichum elongatum* (elongate racomitrium moss).

9-2 *Danthonia californica* (California oatgrass) is the most frequent and dominant grass in this community. It is easily identified by its large spikelets, which usually diverge from the central stalk at a low angle.

9-3 *Festuca roemeri* (Roemer's fescue) is the only non-rhizomatous (i.e., clump-forming) fescue found in these open habitats and is further characterized by grey or glaucous foliage.

9-4 *Achnatherum lemmonii* (Lemmon's needlegrass) has thin and flexible culms. Its spikelets have sharply angled and twisted awns at maturity (inset photo). In contrast, the superficially similar 2-13 *Elymus glaucus* (blue wildrye) always has stiff and straight stems.

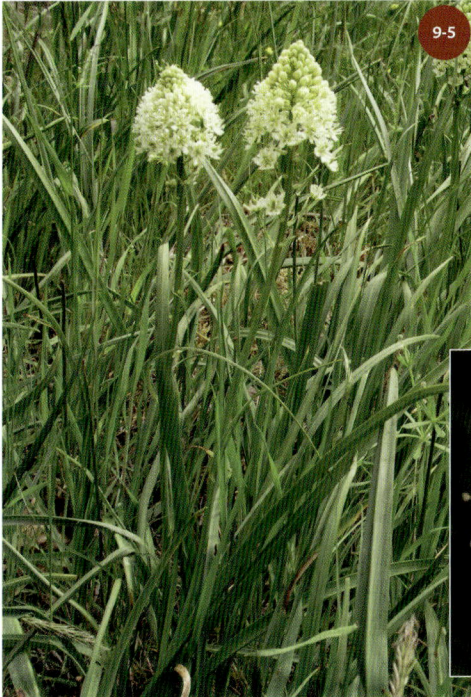

9-5 *Toxicoscordion venenosum* (death camas) is found in both Garry oak (section 7b) and shore pine–Douglas-fir–arbutus woodland (section 8), but it is here, in our pocket grasslands, that it is most frequent. This member of the lily family—well known to Indigenous peoples of the coastal dry belt—is a deadly poisonous plant.

9-6 *Koeleria macrantha* (junegrass) has a narrow cone-shaped inflorescence somewhat resembling that of the introduced *Anthoxanthum odoratum* (sweet vernalgrass). The latter is usually shorter, with flatter, wider leaves and bristly florets.

7-15 *Carex inops* (long-stoloned sedge) usually forms a substantial part of the bio-mass in this community and is therefore pictured here again.

9-7 *Agrostis pallens* (dune bentgrass) grows from strong rhizomes. Its panicle opens only when flowering (inset).

Among the herbaceous species that occur with less than 50 percent frequency in this community, many are familiar to us from the Garry oak realm, including 7-6 *Cerastium arvense* (field chickweed), 7-19 *Trifolium microcephalum* (small-headed clover), 7-34 *Luzula comosa* var. *laxa* (Pacific woodrush), 7-35 *Plectritis congesta* (sea blush), 7-28 *Allium acuminatum* (Hooker's onion), 7-9 *Ranunculus occidentalis* (western buttercup), 7-8 *Delphinium menziesii* (Menzies' larkspur), 7-20 *Trifolium microdon* (thimble clover), 7-24 *Trifolium oliganthum* (few-flowered clover), 7-16 *Primula hendersonii* (broad-leaved shootingstar) and 7-14 *Collinsia parviflora* (small-flowered blue-eyed Mary). A rich, varied and—especially when in bloom—colourful community indeed.

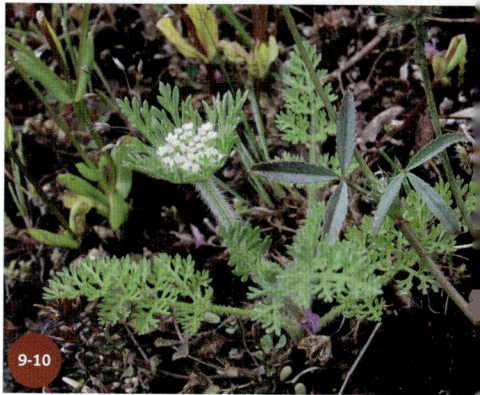

New to us are the following: **9-8 *Madia gracilis* (slender tarweed)** is the larger of the two tarweeds in these grasslands (see 9-28 *Madia exigua*); **9-9 *Leptosiphon minimus* (bicoloured linanthus)**, sometimes called "babystars," is a tiny but attractive species in the *Polemoniaceae* (phlox family), with whorls of leaves and long perianth tubes; **9-10 *Daucus pusillus* (wild carrot)** is another intricate miniature.

Although 9-22 *Primula pauciflora* var. *pauciflora* (pretty shootingstar) does occur in dryer hill-country "balds," it is far more prominent in the wetter seepage sites associated with these grasslands and will be discussed there (section 9b).

9-11 *Clarkia amoena* (farewell-to-spring) flowers, as the common name suggests, when many other plants start to turn yellow after entering summer dormancy. The petals of this species sometimes come with attractive darker spots. This appears to be independent from the two subspecies, ssp. *lindleyi* with narrow stigmatic lobes and ssp. *caurina* with broad lobes, recognized by some sources. The seed pods are flask shaped. (Compare 20-24 *Clarkia purpurea* var. *quadrivulnera*)

9-12 *Triphysaria pusilla* (dwarf owl-clover) comes in two colour forms, one with dark purple pigment and almost black flowers (pictured here) and another one with greenish pigment and yellow flowers.

9-13 *Microsteris gracilis* (slender phlox) is another small member of the *Polemoniaceae*. It is an annual, like dwarf owl-clover, farewell-to-spring, wild carrot, bicoloured linanthus and slender tarweed, and must grow back from seed each year.

9-14 *Prunella vulgaris* (self-heal) is a perennial member of the mint family (*Lamiaceae*).

9-15 *Agoseris grandiflora* (large-flowered agoseris) is the larger and perennial member of this genus. A dandelion relative, it usually grows in the cracks of rocks scattered in these grasslands.

9-16 *Castilleja attenuata* (narrow-leaved paintbrush), an annual formerly classified as an owl-clover, is closely related to 9-12 *Triphysaria pusilla*.

9-17 *Agoseris heterophylla* (annual agoseris) is the smaller sibling of the species described above (see 9-15). Its leaves may be entire or lobed. If entire, it could be confused with the non-native *Hypochaeris glabra* (smooth cat's-ear).

9-18 *Perideridia montana* (common yampah) is a tall, thin-stemmed plant in the parsley family (*Apiaceae*) whose leaves appear in early spring and may show amazing variation, from fennel-like to parsnip-like shapes, as shown. Flowering does not occur until mid to late summer. Its tuber-like roots were eaten by Indigenous peoples.

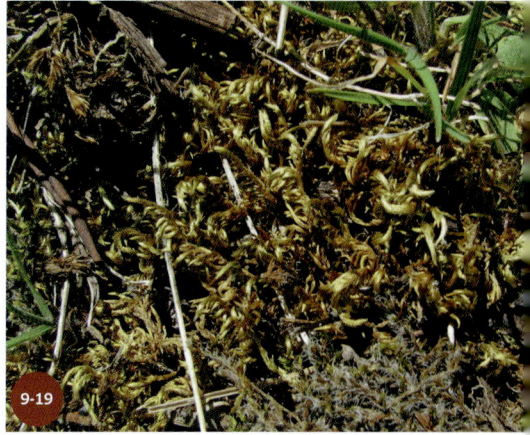

In the moss layer, the dominant species is again 7-30 *Niphotrichum elongatum* (elongate racomitrium moss).

9-19 *Homalothecium aeneum* (golden curly moss)—shown here when dry—also occurs in half of all sites. This moss is like a miniature version of 8-7 *Homalothecium megaptilum* (trachybryum moss), which grows in the adjacent shore pine–Douglas-fir–arbutus woodland under shore pine.

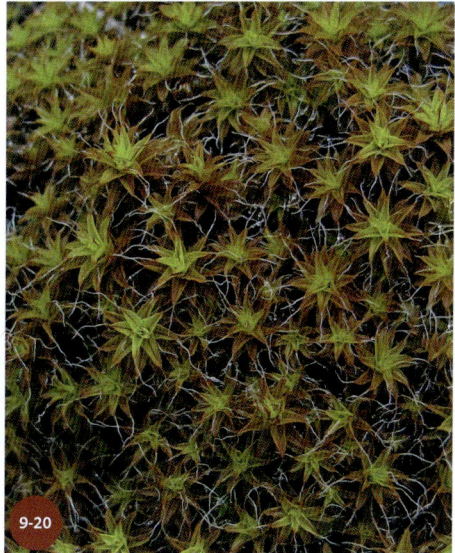

Also present is **9-20 *Syntrichia ruralis* (hair screw-moss)**, shown left when dry and right when wet. 8-6 *Polytrichum juniperinum* (juniper haircap moss) and 8-5 *Dicranum scoparium* (broom moss), already known to us from earlier listings, are found in less than one third of the sampled stands of this community.

9b Shallow Soil Seepage Sites within Pocket Grasslands

Some of the most colourful and floristically interesting plant combinations occur in hill-country habitats that are under the influence of seepage. These are generally very shallow soils over slanting rock surfaces or sometimes only moss-covered rocks. Excess moisture is usually limited to spring, and the sites dry out in late spring or early summer.

Only three species in this habitat are familiar to us from previous sections: 9-2 *Danthonia californica* (California oatgrass), 7-11 *Triteleia hyacinthina* (white triteleia) and 9-14 *Prunella vulgaris* (self-heal).

Table 9b: Shallow Soil Seepage Sites within Pocket Grasslands

Herb Layer	%
Danthonia californica (California oatgrass)	100
Erythranthe microphylla (small-leaved monkeyflower)	82
Triteleia hyacinthina (white triteleia)	82
Primula pauciflora var. *pauciflora* (pretty shootingstar)	71
Aspidotis densa (dense lace fern)	53
Trifolium variegatum (white-tipped clover)	53
Heterocodon rariflorus (heterocodon)	47
Prunella vulgaris (self-heal)	47
Allium amplectens (slim-leaf onion)	29
Dichanthelium acuminatum (western witchgrass)	29

Herb Layer	%
Agrostis microphylla (dwarf bentgrass)	24
Madia exigua (little tarweed)	24

Moss Layer	%
Imbribryum miniatum (glossy red bryum moss)	65
Codriophorus acicularis (needle-leaved fringe moss)	24

Non-native
Bromus racemosus (bald brome)

> 75% chance of seeing this species
50–75% chance of seeing this species
25–49% chance of seeing this species
< 25% chance of seeing this species

The large flowers of **9-21 *Erythranthe microphylla* (small-leaved monkeyflower)** make seepage sites stand out from a distance.

9-22 *Primula pauciflora* var. *pauciflora* (pretty shootingstar) differs from 7-16 *Primula hendersonii* (inset) by having narrower elongated leaves and a yellow ring around the base of the stamen tube.

9-23 *Dichanthelium acuminatum* **(western witchgrass)** is related to millet (genus *Panicum*) and used to bear this generic name until re-classified.

9-24 *Aspidotis densa* **(dense lace fern)** and **9-25** *Heterocodon rariflorus* **(heterocodon)** both like the shelter of rocks. To see flowers on the latter is rare, as indicated in the specific name *rariflorus*.

9-26 *Trifolium variegatum* (white-tipped clover), **9-28 *Madia exigua* (little tarweed)** and **9-29 *Agrostis microphylla* (dwarf bentgrass)** are small annuals that prefer wet ground. The latter is often only a few centimetres tall.

9-27 Allium amplectens (slim-leaf onion) grows from a 6-to-8-millimetre-diameter spherical bulb. Its leaves are narrow and thread-like, and its attractive flowers are white or pale pink. It is classified as rare.

In the moss layer, **9-30 Imbribryum miniatum (glossy red bryum moss)** stands out because of its brilliant colours. A frequent associate is **9-31 Codriophorus acicularis (needle-leaved fringe moss)**. Despite the name, its leaf tips are rounded!

NATIVE PLANTS OF WETLANDS AND COASTAL HABITATS

IN THE PREVIOUS SECTIONS OF THIS GUIDE, NATIVE PLANTS WERE PRESENTED within the framework of analyzed plant communities. This allowed us to calculate a percent frequency for each species within a community (approximately how likely each species is to occur) on the basis of pre-existing data. With the exception of Table 10, such data were not available to the authors for wetlands and coastal habitats. Still, an effort has been made to list individual species in the sequence from most to least frequent. However, this is based on observations and informal notes rather than on calculated frequencies.

The plant communities described here are generally more broadly defined than those based on percent frequency data. As this component of the guide encompasses greater habitat diversity, it was necessary to add more detail to the conditions under which individual species occur. For instance, more sedges are listed for marshes than would ordinarily be found growing together in a single marsh. This is because the different types of marshes that exist cannot all be individually detailed within this guide.

This part of the guide deals with a variety of wetland habitats, beach habitats, sand dunes and coastal bluffs. All are habitats that are naturally uncommon in the coastal dry belt or that have become uncommon in their original form due to human activities in and on these landscapes. Alteration due to human activity is particularly true for wetlands.

The main types of wetlands encountered in our area are shrub-covered swamps, marshes and bogs. (Fens are nearly absent from the dry belt.) Of these, bogs have suffered the greatest losses and changes. Occurrences of their most important constituents, peat mosses (*Sphagnum* spp.), are now quite rare.

In a forest-dominated landscape, wetlands were important to early colonists as pastures for livestock until larger tracts could be cleared of trees. Virtually all wetlands experienced attempts at draining them. The majority of wetlands we see today have secondarily regenerated after such attempts at drainage, many of them with the help of beavers.

In those wetlands where beavers were or still are a factor, the time since the last beaver activity is also an important determinant of plant species combinations and species richness, as successional development catches up with changing water levels. Low species diversity and the preponderance of aquatic vegetation on recently flooded land will normally be replaced by higher species diversity and less aquatic vegetation as the water level stabilizes.

10 Shrub-covered Wetlands

How do you recognize these wetlands?

These are shrub communities on wet ground. Shrub-covered swamps are the most common wetland habitat in the coastal dry belt.

Water tables in swamp habitat are high but fluctuate considerably between the wet seasons and late summer. In winter the roots and lower parts of the shrubs are generally submerged, and the water level drops just enough during the summer to expose the base of the shrubs and some of the roots. Surface soils are black and muddy and remain moist and soft even in summer. Shrub growth is generally dense, usually to the extent that herbaceous species, mosses and liverworts are either scattered or absent.

Table 10 lists the species combination for this habitat. The image below shows two manifestations of shrub-covered swamps. The simplest form of this community consisting entirely of 5-8 *Spiraea douglasii* (hardhack) is seen in the foreground. A more complex mixed stand of taller shrubs, including willows, is in the right background. *Spiraea douglasii* is also present in the mixed, more diverse vegetation.

Taller, mixed shrubs

5-8

5-3

Table 10: Shrub-covered Wetlands

Shrub & Tree Layer	%
Spiraea douglasii (hardhack)	100
Cornus sericea (red-osier dogwood)	83
Salix sitchensis (Sitka willow)	78
Salix lasiandra (Pacific willow)	70
Malus fusca (Pacific crab apple)	48
Salix hookeriana (Hooker's willow)	48
Salix geyeriana (Geyer's willow)	39
Alnus rubra (red alder)	35
Physocarpus capitatus (Pacific ninebark)	26
Rubus spectabilis (salmonberry)	13
Lonicera involucrata (black twinberry)	9
Frangula purshiana (cascara)	9
Rosa pisocarpa (clustered wild rose)	9
Salix scouleriana (Scouler's willow)	9

Moss Layer	%
Kindbergia praelonga (slender beaked-moss)	26
Leptodictyum riparium (e.g., aquamoss)	17
Rhizomnium glabrescens (large leafy moss)	9

Non-native
Phalaris arundinacea (reed canarygrass)
Juncus effusus (common rush, European forms)
Ranunculus repens (creeping buttercup)

Herb Layer	%
Carex obnupta (slough sedge)	39
Lysichiton americanus (skunk cabbage)	39
Athyrium filix-femina (lady fern)	22
Lycopus uniflorus (northern water horehound)	17
Oenanthe sarmentosa (Pacific water-parsley)	17
Veronica beccabunga var. *americana* (American speedwell)	17
Galium trifidum (small bedstraw)	13
Scirpus microcarpus (small-flowered bulrush)	13
Torreyochloa pallida var. *pauciflora* (weak false-manna)	13
Carex canescens (grey sedge)	9
Carex leptopoda (short-scaled sedge)	9
Comarum palustre (marsh cinquefoil)	9
Eleocharis palustris (common spike-rush)	9
Mentha canadensis (Canada mint)	9
Myosotis laxa (small-flowered forget-me-not)	9
Sium suave (hemlock water-parsnip)	9
Typha latifolia (common cattail)	9
Veronica scutellata (marsh speedwell)	9

> 75% chance of seeing this species
50–75% chance of seeing this species
25–49% chance of seeing this species
< 25% chance of seeing this species

After 5-8 *Spiraea douglasii* (hardhack), the second most frequent species in our shrub-covered wetlands, 5-3 *Cornus sericea* (red-osier dogwood), is familiar to us from the black cottonwood community.

It is followed by several willow species, introduced here for the first time: 10-1 *Salix sitchensis* (Sitka willow); 10-2 *Salix lasiandra* (Pacific willow); 10-3 *Salix hookeriana* (Hooker's willow); and 10-4 *Salix geyeriana* (Geyer's willow).

5-8 *Spiraea douglasii* (hardhack).

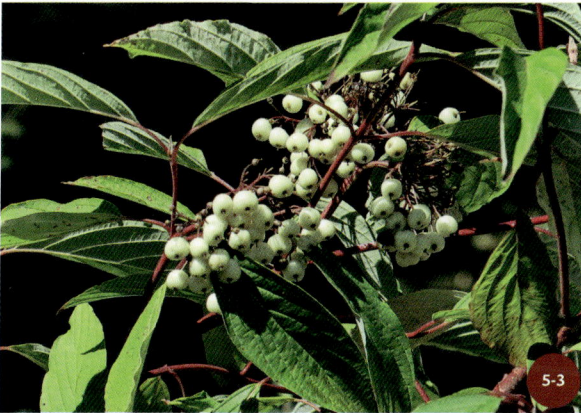

5-3 *Cornus sericea* (red-osier dogwood).

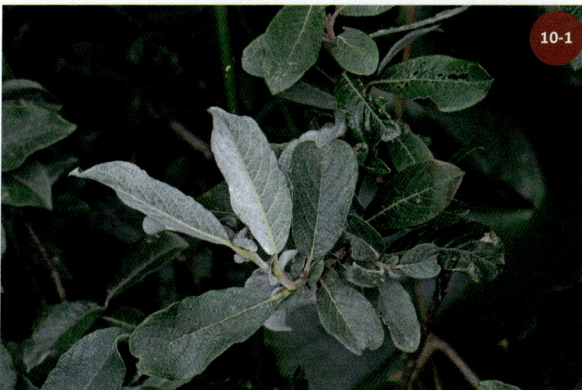

10-1 *Salix sitchensis* (Sitka willow) is similar to 2-2 *Salix scouleriana* (Scouler's willow) but is distinguished by its shiny, satin-like pubescence (soft down) on the underside of the leaves. In wet habitats like the one pictured, *Salix scouleriana* is usually absent.

10-2 *Salix lasiandra* (Pacific willow) is the tallest of the wetland willows and has a long leaf with a gradually tapered leaf tip.

5-4 *Malus fusca* (Pacific crab apple) occurs in about one half of all stands of this community

5-4 *Malus fusca* (Pacific crab apple) and **10-3 Salix hookeriana (Hooker's willow)** both occur in about one half of all stands of this community. *Salix hookeriana* is distinguished by large leaves that are densely covered with soft hair and borne on stiffer, more upright branches than is typical for other willows.

Another willow encountered in fewer than half of the samples is **10-4 Salix geyeriana (Geyer's willow)**. This willow has sharply pointed leaves that are smaller than 10-2 *Salix lasiandra* (Pacific willow) but without the long, tapering leaf tip. Its branches are also more slender than those of other willows.

Other species that are occasionally found in shrub-covered swamps are 4-1 *Alnus rubra* (red alder), 5-7 *Physocarpus capitatus* (Pacific ninebark), 3-4 *Rubus spectabilis* (salmonberry), 5-5 *Lonicera involucrata* (black twinberry), 1-15 *Frangula purshiana* (cascara) and 5-9 *Rosa pisocarpa* (clustered wild rose), all of them familiar from previous sections of this guide.

Some examples of this community lack a herbaceous layer because the density of shrubs will not always allow it. When present, scattered individuals of 5-11 *Carex obnupta* (slough sedge), 4-6 *Lysichiton americanus* (skunk cabbage) and/or 4-5 *Athyrium filix-femina* (lady fern) may be found in one quarter to one third of the stands.

Additional herbaceous species that remain in Table 10 are almost all plants of more open habitats such as marshes and will be examined in the next section.

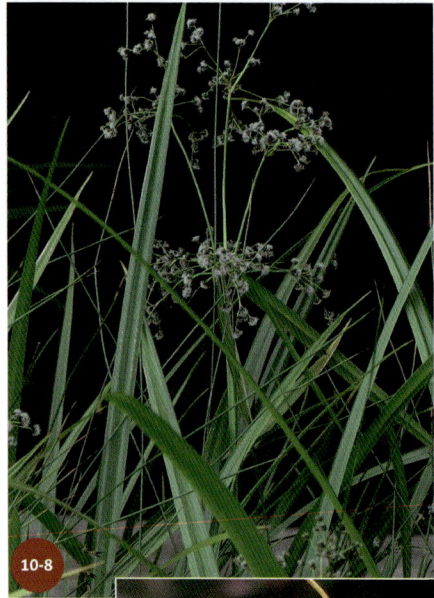

Less frequent still are 4-13 *Oenanthe sarmentosa*
(Pacific water-parsley) and 4-15 *Torreyochloa pallida*
var. *pauciflora* (weak false-manna). Equally sporadic
are **10-5 *Lycopus uniflorus* (northern water horehound),
10-6 *Veronica beccabunga* var. *americana*
(American speedwell), 10-7 *Galium trifidum*
(small bedstraw) and 10-8 *Scirpus microcarpus*
(small-flowered bulrush).**

Due to shrub density, mosses are equally as sporadic here as herbaceous plants. Only one, 3-13 *Kindbergia praelonga* (slender beaked-moss), occurs in about one quarter of all stands. 11-28 *Leptodictyum riparium* (sometimes used as an aquarium plant, e.g., aquamoss) occurs more frequently in marsh environments (section 11).

Marshes

How do you recognize this type of wetland?

In our context, a marsh is a wetland with herbaceous plant cover but without any woody plants.

Marshes occur in many different forms and species combinations, depending on soil, nutrient and water conditions. Average water levels are important determinants, but water level fluctuations between wet and dry seasons are equally decisive for their species combination.

The following list combines the most frequently encountered species in these various forms of marshes. Species are grouped to facilitate comparison between related species.

Here we see a marsh with **11-1 *Typha latifolia* (common cattail)**. This marsh, originally dominated by native sedges, has been invaded by the non-native form of *Phalaris arundinacea* (reed canarygrass), an aggressive grass that is now common in all wetland communities.

Table 11: List of Frequent Marsh Species

Sedges

Carex cusickii (Cusick's sedge)

Carex exsiccata (inflated sedge)

Carex utriculata (beaked sedge)

Carex obnupta (slough sedge)

Carex sitchensis (Sitka sedge)

*Carex lasiocarp*a (slender sedge)

Sedge Relatives

Dulichium arundinaceum (three-way sedge)

Eleocharis palustris (common spike-rush)

Scirpus microcarpus
(small-flowered bulrush)

Rushes

Juncus effusus ssp. (common rush)

Juncus articulatus (jointed rush)

Juncus supiniformis (spreading rush)

Juncus acuminatus (tapered rush)

Juncus ensifolius (dagger-leaf rush)

Grasses

Torreyochloa pallida var. *pauciflora*
(weak false-manna)

Agrostis scabra (hair bentgrass)

Glyceria grandis (reed mannagrass)

Glyceria elata (tall mannagrass)

Other Monocots

Sparganium emersum (emersed bur-reed)

Typha latifolia (common cattail)

Lysichiton americanus (skunk cabbage)

Shrubs

Spiraea douglasii (hardhack)

Other Herbaceous Plants

Lycopus uniflorus
(northern water horehound)

Scutellaria lateriflora (blue skullcap)

Galium trifidum (small bedstraw)

Oenanthe sarmentosa (Pacific water-parsley)

Veronica scutellata (marsh speedwell)

Myosotis laxa
(small-flowered forget-me-not)

Comarum palustre (marsh cinquefoil)

Epilobium ciliatum
(purple-leaved willowherb)

Mentha canadensis (Canada mint)

Lysimachia thyrsiflora (tufted loosestrife)

Hypericum anagalloides
(bog St. John's-wort)

Stellaria borealis ssp. *sitchana*
(boreal starwort)

Persicaria amphibia (water smartweed)

Veronica beccabunga var. *americana*
(American speedwell)

Non-native

Phalaris arundinacea (reed canarygrass)

Iris pseudacorus (yellow iris)

Juncus effusus ssp.
(European forms of common rush)

Sedges are the classical marsh plants and usually contribute the largest biomass to marsh vegetation. The following species are the most frequent and often also the most abundant in marshes. However, it is rare that more than three, or at most four, sedge species co-occur in any one marsh. In fact, a single species frequently dominates the community, as with 11-6 *Carex lasiocarpa* (slender sedge) forming pure stands in shallow water.

All six sedge species described here are large plants, well over half a metre tall and often much taller.

The photograph above is of a marsh with large, patchy stands of 11-2 *Carex cusickii* (Cusick's sedge), 11-3 *Carex utriculata* (beaked sedge), 11-4 *Carex sitchensis* (Sitka sedge) and *Phalaris arundinacea* (reed canarygrass).

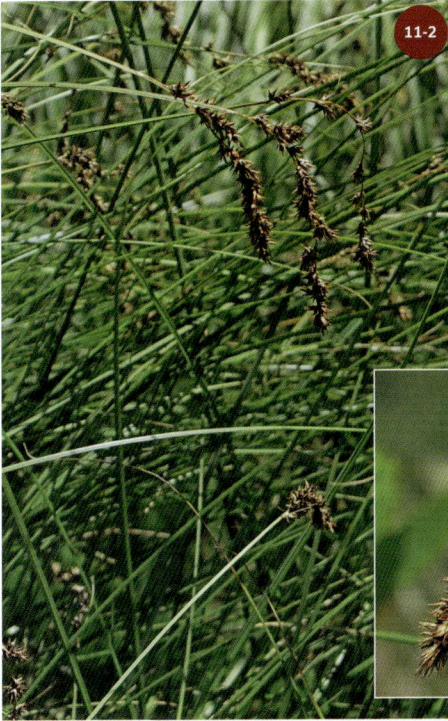

11-2 *Carex cusickii* **(Cusick's sedge)** has a compound multi-branched inflorescence more reminiscent of a grass inflorescence and has long, narrow leaves that grow in clumps. The remaining five sedges all have inflorescences with dissimilar male and female spikes, with the male spikes borne on top.

11-5 *Carex exsiccata* **(inflated sedge)** is another species that tends to clump. It has a fewer-flowered female spike than the other species.

11-3

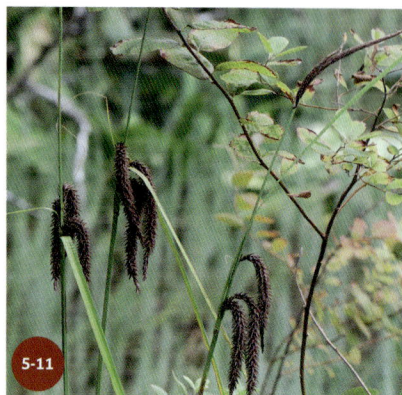

5-11

11-3 *Carex utriculata* (beaked sedge) is similar but grows from rhizomes, thus develops stands with evenly spaced shoots.

5-11 *Carex obnupta* (slough sedge), first introduced to us in the black cottonwood community (section 5), also grows from rhizomes and forms large even stands. It has dark green leaves, and the unstalked female spikes have a characteristic drooping habit at maturity. This sedge is more common in lightly treed wetlands than in open marshes.

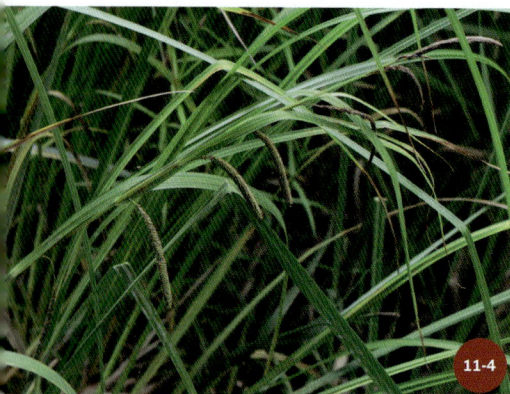

11-4

11-4 *Carex sitchensis* (Sitka sedge) also has drooping spikes, but these (at least the lower ones) are borne on thin stalks. The fruits of the female spikes (perigynia) are smaller and more crowded than in the other species.

11-6

11-6 *Carex lasiocarpa* (slender sedge) is tall and slender with narrow leaves and short spikes. The perigynia are hairy. This is another rhizomatous species and is, as mentioned earlier, usually found growing in shallow water.

11-7

11-8

There are three sedge-related plants (members of the *Cyperaceae* family) frequent in marshes and in shallow water on the edge of ponds and lakes. The first, **11-7 *Dulichium arundinaceum* (three-way sedge)**, has a very different architecture, with leaf blades all along the stem and bundles of spikes arising from the leaf axils.

Another sedge-related plant, **11-8 *Eleocharis palustris* (common spike-rush)**, has a straight, unbranched, leafless stem terminating in a simple spike.

The third member of the *Cyperaceae* family was introduced to us in shrub-covered wetlands (section 10). 10-8 *Scirpus microcarpus* (small-flowered bulrush) is a leafier plant than other members of this genus. It is unmistakable due to its broad double-folded leaves. In fact, without the large spreading inflorescence, the leaves could be mistaken for those of a large sedge. Note that an even larger plant in this genus, *Scirpus atrocinctus* (wool-grass, not pictured), with tall but narrow leaves, also occurs sporadically in beaver swamps.

The five species of *Juncus* (rushes) named in the list (p. 121) can cause some confusion. **11-9 *Juncus effusus* (common rush)** is a large, clumped, ubiquitous species. It may be split into numerous sub-species or varieties. The taxonomic classification of introduced and native North American *Juncus effusus* is difficult and not universally agreed upon by expert botanists. It is challenging to distinguish the different forms in the field. Here we must treat them as one unit, which requires also listing them among non-native plants.

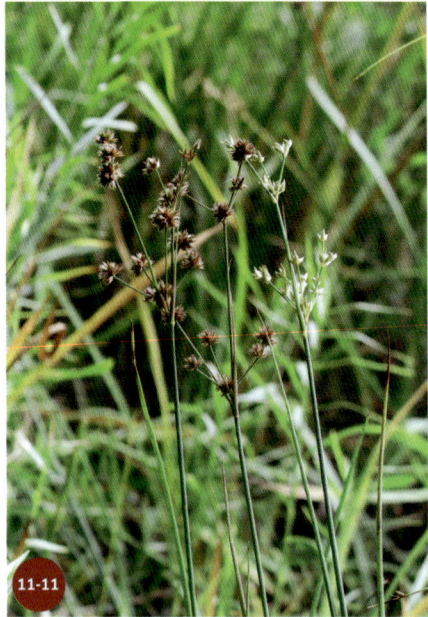

The following four *Juncus* species are in a group of rushes that have septate leaves (septate means divided by cross-walls). The cross-walls can be felt when pulling the leaf between two fingers. They are visible in image 11-10. Two similar species occur scattered in marshes, **11-10 *Juncus articulatus* (jointed rush)** and **11-11 *Juncus acuminatus* (tapered rush)**. In 11-10 *Juncus articulatus* (jointed rush) the seed capsules are longer, and in 11-11 *Juncus acuminatus* (tapered rush) they are shorter than or equal to the flowers. *Juncus acuminatus* tends to have more flowers per cluster than *Juncus articulatus*.

The terrestrial form of **11-12 *Juncus supiniformis* (spreading rush)** can be deceivingly similar to *Juncus articulatus*, as shown in the photo. *Juncus supiniformis* is more often an aquatic plant and will also be covered in the next section. However, in dry summers when its habitat dries out, it assumes an upright growth form that resembles *Juncus articulatus*. In those cases, the viviparous florets (11-12 inset) and the frequent rooting of the basal parts from the nodes are helpful as distinctions.

Among native grasses, only one species, 4-15 *Torreyochloa pallida* var. *pauciflora* (weak false-manna), is frequent in marshes. It never forms large clumps or stands but occurs as widely scattered individuals (an example of a frequent but not abundant plant).

11-13 *Juncus ensifolius* (dagger-leaf rush) is the fourth common species with jointed leaves occasionally found in marshes and adjacent habitats. As the common name suggests, the leaves of this rush are flat and positioned with the sharp edge toward the stem in iris-fashion. The inflorescences are ball shaped.

While rarely growing in open marshes, two species of manna grasses often command attention, one by its giant size and the other by its frequency in wet habitats. The first, **11-14 *Glyceria grandis* (reed mannagrass)**, can reach 150 to 200 centimetres. It is one of the tallest native grasses, with an impressively large pyramidal inflorescence and lush green leaves. It grows from rhizomes in sloughs and other nutrient-rich sites and often forms stands of non-flowering leafy plants, with just a few of the giant fertile plants scattered about. The second, **11-15 *Glyceria elata* (tall mannagrass)**, despite its name, is only about two thirds the size of reed mannagrass. It is a frequent inhabitant of wet openings in red alder stands and similar wet sites along shaded water courses. This species also shows a tendency for lush green non-flowering vegetative shoots with a characteristic fan-shaped architecture (as pictured) typical for the species. Both these mannagrasses, as well as most other species in the genus, have rounded or blunt flowering parts, with the individual flowering or fruiting scales prominently ridged longitudinally (inset photos).

Curiously, a grass that is frequent on dry, barren rock outcrops, **11-16 *Agrostis scabra* (hair bentgrass)**, may also be found in marshes and attains a much larger size in these wet environments. It has a large, widely spreading inflorescence composed of thin hair-like branches and minute spikelets.

We have looked at sedges, sedge-related species, rushes and grasses, all monocoty-ledons (monocots) that grow in marshes, but there are three more marsh plants in this group: common cattail, skunk cabbage and bur-reed.

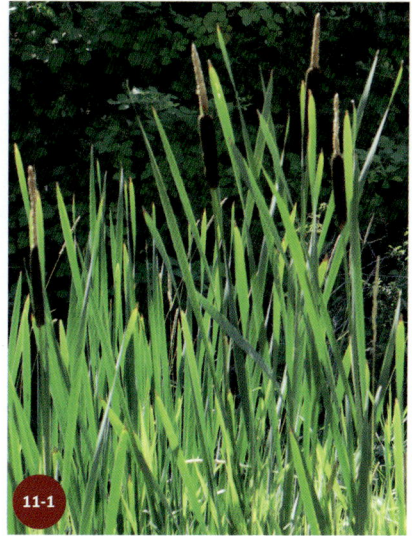

11-1 *Typha latifolia* (common cattail) is an important and conspicuous marsh plant.

11-17 *Sparganium emersum* (emersed bur-reed) is one of two locally common bur-reeds and is a frequent component of marsh vegetation. *Sparganium natans*, the other bur-reed, is presented in the next section.

Introduced in section 4, 4-6 *Lysichiton americanus* (skunk cabbage) is another well-known species encountered in other wetlands and wet forests. It is consistently scattered among marsh vegetation.

The following common marsh plants are herbaceous dicotyledons (dicots) that are usually scattered among the more dominant monocots such as sedges and cattails.

10-5 *Lycopus uniflorus* (northern water horehound), already encountered in the previous section (see p. 118), is probably the most frequent species in this group. It is distinguished from other native species by having rounded rather than spine-tipped calyx lobes.

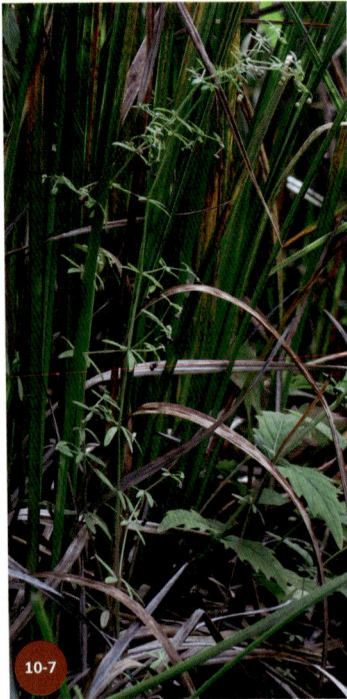

10-7 *Galium trifidum* (small bedstraw), also described previously, is pictured again, this time as a fruiting specimen.

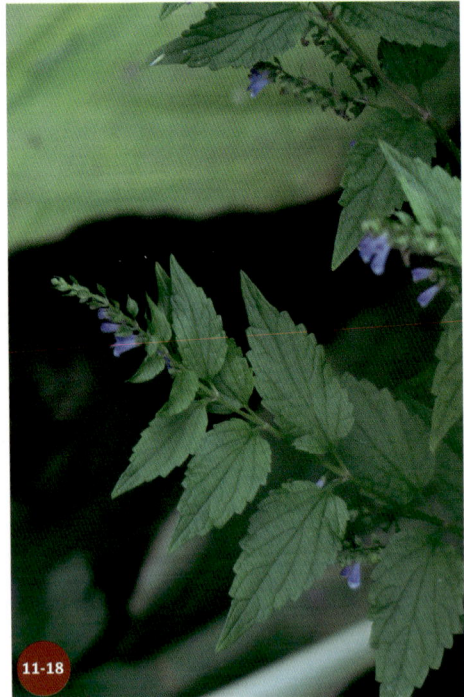

11-18 *Scutellaria lateriflora* (blue skullcap) is a smaller-flowered and more common relative of marsh skullcap (not pictured).

4-13 *Oenanthe sarmentosa* (Pacific water-parsley) is equally frequent here as in several other wet plant communities already discussed.

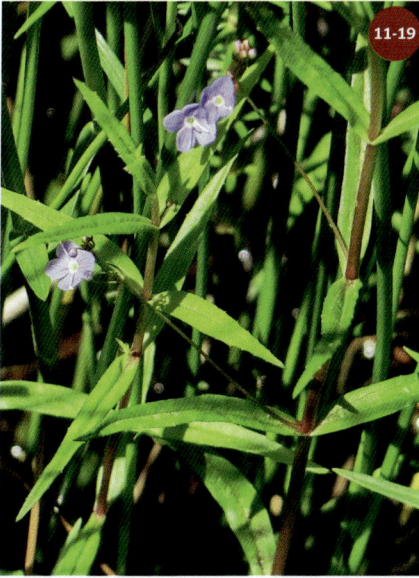

Two species of *Veronica* are part of this group, 10-6 *Veronica beccabunga* var. *americana* (American speedwell) and more commonly **11-19 Veronica scutellata (marsh speedwell)**. The latter often grows in standing water and has long, lax shoots supported by other tall marsh plants.

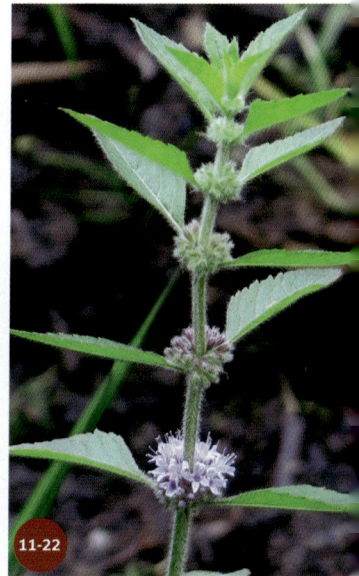

11-20 Myosotis laxa (small-flowered forget-me-not), 11-21 Comarum palustre (marsh cinquefoil) and **11-22 Mentha canadensis (Canada mint)** all occur with lower frequency in Table 10 (Shrub-covered Wetlands). They come into their own in this brighter, more open marsh environment.

11-23 *Hypericum anagalloides* (bog St. John's-wort) is diminutive compared to other species in this genus. It occurs both under the tall vegetation of marshes and in the more open environment of bogs.

11-24 *Stellaria borealis* ssp. *sitchana* (boreal starwort) is a delicate member of the pink family, with small white flowers. It will grow to 70 centimetres or more when the thin stems get support from tall sedges and reeds in marshes.

11-25 *Lysimachia thyrsiflora* (tufted loosestrife) has small yellow flowers bundled in ball-shaped axillary inflorescences. It is a member of the primrose family and stands in shallow water while in bloom.

11-26 *Persicaria amphibia* (water smartweed) occurs both as a semi-terrestrial marsh plant and as a largely aquatic plant on which only the flowers and two or three floating leaves appear above the surface.

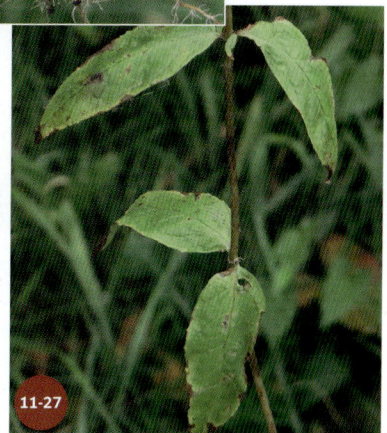

Some tall plants with small flowers require two or more images to show their characteristic features. This is certainly the case for **11-27 *Epilobium ciliatum* (purple-leaved willowherb)**. A tall plant, much branched above, often reaching one metre or more in height, it is frequent in marshes with sedges and cattail.

Wet marshes that dry out at the end of dry summers almost always have a considerable component of those aquatic plants that can survive in a more terrestrial form, such as yellow pond lily (12-1 *Nuphar polysepalum*), American water plantain (12-7 *Alisma triviale*) and even some pondweeds. These will be dealt with in the upcoming section on emergent aquatic plant habitats.

5-8

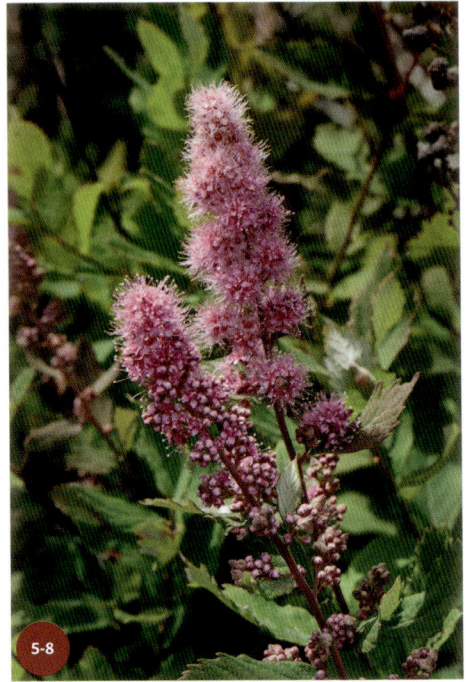

11-28

Many of the species covered in this section could be discussed in either marshes or aquatic habitats. While marshes by definition are generally free of woody plants, there are few that lack scattered individuals or small clumps of the ubiquitous 5-8 *Spiraea douglasii* (hardhack).

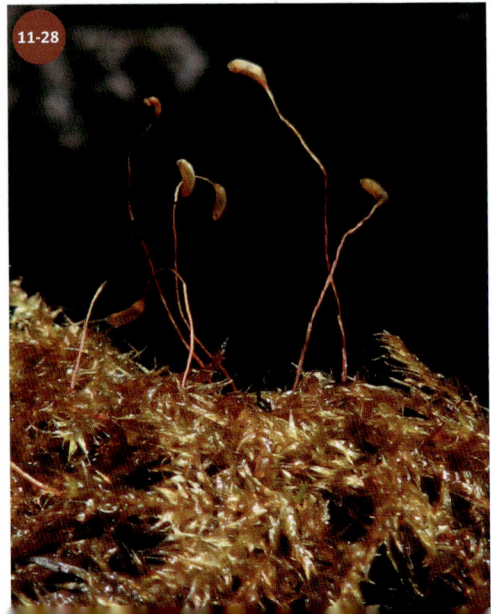

11-28

The bryophyte flora of marshes varies considerably. As in the adjacent shrub-covered wetlands, **11-28 Leptodictyum riparium (e.g., aquamoss)** is often present. However, it must not be confused with similar *Fontinalis* mosses, which are larger and tend to occur in the moving water of streams. *L. riparium* can also be confused with other wet-habitat mosses that have sideways-curved (falcate) leaves.

12 Floating Leaf and Emergent Aquatic Plant Habitats

How do you recognize these habitats?

This section deals with plants that grow in the water but have conspicuous above-surface parts that can be observed from shore or from a boat. We haven't included aquatic species in this guide, because they are difficult to observe, describe and identify, and a challenge to photograph adequately.

Some species listed here as emergent aquatic plants can also occur in the wettest parts of marshes (e.g., 11-26 *Persicaria amphibia*). They usually have submerged parts that differ in morphological structure from their emergent or floating parts. A good example of this is seen in image 12-4 *Potamogeton amplifolius* (large-leaved pondweed).

As is characteristic for plants in these habitats, 12-5 *Potamogeton gramineus* (grass-leaved pondweed), 12-9 *Hippuris vulgaris* (common mare's tail), 12-11 *Sparganium natans* (small bur-reed) and 11-12 *Juncus supiniformis* (spreading rush) all exhibit morphological differences between submerged and emergent or floating parts.

This image shows a frequent near-shore zonation along the shore of a small lake with floating-leaf plants and a dense belt of **12-6 *Schoenoplectus acutus* (hard-stemmed bulrush)**.

A closer view of a mixed floating-leaf community is inset, with **12-1 *Nuphar polysepalum* (yellow pond lily)**, **12-2 *Brasenia schreberi* (water shield)** and **12-3 *Potamogeton natans* (floating-leaved pondweed)**.

In the larger illustration of **12-1 *Nuphar polysepalum* (yellow pond lily)**, a specimen with raised leaves is shown surrounded by floating leaves. Leaf stalks and flowering stems arise from the top end of a large and often very long rhizome. The upright leaves occur where the rhizome reaches close to the surface and can support them.

12-2 *Brasenia schreberi* (water shield) is special among native plants in having leaf stalks centrally attached to the leaf's undersurface. Leaf and flowering stalks in *Brasenia* are enveloped in a layer of mucus secreted by special hairs on these stalks. This is visible as a whitish layer along the stalks in our photo. When handled, the mucus layer makes the plants quite slippery.

The genus *Potamogeton* (pondweeds) comprises a large number of different species. Only the three that are common in our area are shown here: **12-4 *Potamogeton amplifolius* (large-leaved pondweed)**, **12-3 *Potamogeton natans* (floating-leaved pondweed)** and **12-5 *Potamogeton gramineus* (grass-leaved pondweed)**. Grass-leaved pondweed has smaller floating leaves than the other two. Its common name refers to the shape of the submerged leaves.

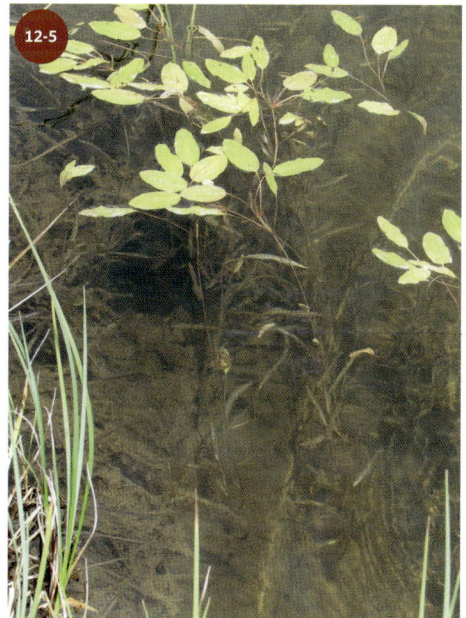

In lakes and ponds of our area, **12-6** *Schoenoplectus acutus* **(hard-stemmed bulrush)** is the more common of two very similar species. The other species, 18-16 *Schoenoplectus tabernaemontani* (soft-stemmed bulrush), is sometimes found in brackish waters or in other mineral-rich sites. Its main difference is the spongier tissue of the stem, as described by its common name. 12-6 *Schoenoplectus acutus* tends to form dense, pure stands in water between 0.5 and 1 metre deep.

12-6

12-7

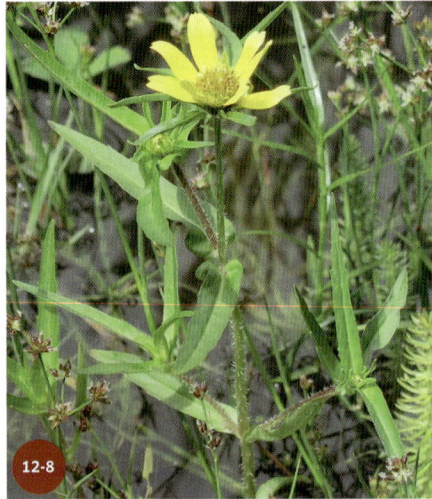
12-8

12-7 *Alisma triviale* **(American water plantain)** grows in shallow water near the edge of ponds and lakes. This is another species that could be listed either as a marsh plant or an aquatic. However, in our area it is not a frequent component of marshes. The same could be said of **12-8** *Bidens cernua* **(nodding beggarticks)**, which normally grows in standing water, at least in the spring and summer before some of its habitats dry up. Of several species in this genus, this is the only one common in our area. *Bidens amplissima* (Vancouver Island beggarticks, not pictured) is a local rarity and is distinguished by its three-lobed leaves.

12-9 _Hippuris vulgaris_ (common mare's tail) has two very different growth forms. The aquatic form is soft and flowing, hence its common name. It is visible in image 12-10 to the left of the blooms. The above-water form of 12-9 is stiffly upright.

The attractive yellow bloom in this photo belongs to **12-10 _Utricularia macrorhiza_ (greater bladderwort)**, a carnivorous aquatic plant. The second, smaller 12-10 image shows part of a bladderwort shoot with numerous "bladders" that can produce a sudden vacuum, thereby sucking in and trapping tiny crustaceans and other small creatures for digestion. This is the largest and most common of the five species native to the province.

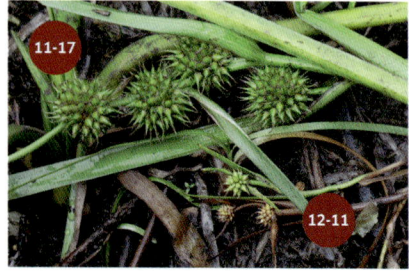

Another species of bur-reed frequent in our area is **12-11 *Sparganium natans* (small bur-reed)**. It has a more aquatic habit than 11-17 *Sparganium emersum* (emersed bur-reed), which is common as an upright marsh plant. Small bur-reed has lax, submerged leaves, with just occasional leaves floating on the surface. Additional images under 12-11 show the less beaked fruit of small bur-reed. Compare the size of the fruiting heads of the two species.

Occasionally, a small aquatic buttercup may be observed in ponds, ditches and lakes. This is **12-12 *Ranunculus flammula* (lesser spearwort**, the plant shown being **var. *ovalis***). Other aquatic species of *Ranunculus* are plants of flowing waters, a special habitat not covered in this guide.

In section 11 (Marshes) we were introduced to 11-12 *Juncus supiniformis* (spreading rush). It can occur in a variety of growth forms and habitats. Here it is shown as an aquatic plant with only its flowering parts above the surface of the water.

Thus far we have looked at floating leaf plants that are anchored by roots in a substrate on the bottom of a water body. There is a league of floating leaf plants that lack such anchoring and float freely. Among them are the duckweeds.

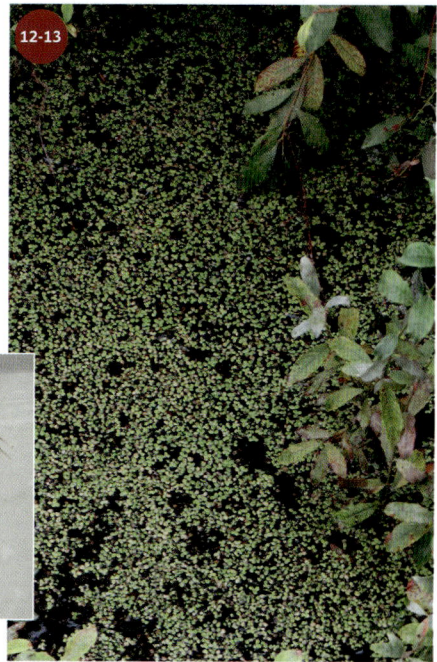

12-13 *Spirodela polyrhiza* (great duckweed) shows a pond covered with this plant. A few specimens of **12-14 *Lemna minor* (common duckweed)** are scattered among them. Despite its name, great duckweed grows to only 5 millimetres across, while common duckweed, at 3 to 4 millimetres across, is even smaller. The detailed photograph shows four *Spirodela* (12-13) plants on the left and two *Lemna* (12-14) plants on the right. The inset 12-13 image shows the red undersurface of *Spirodela polyrhiza*.

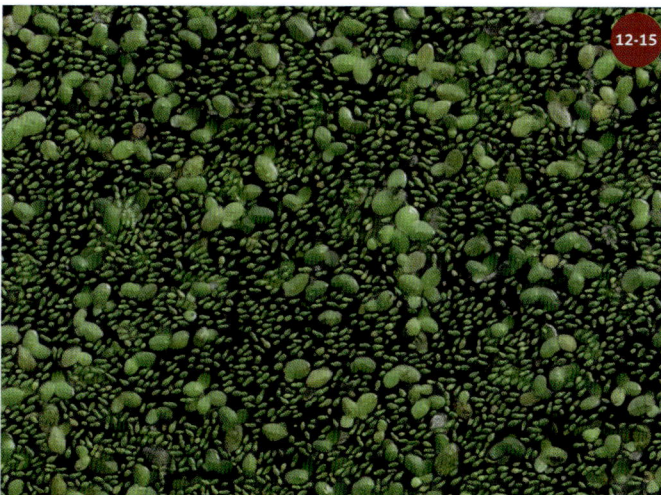

The ultimate in small size is **12-15 *Wolffia borealis* (northern water-meal)**, averaging about 0.7 of a millimetre long. Here it is shown between larger *Lemna minor* plants.

13 **Peat Bogs**

How do you recognize peat bogs?

The defining feature of peat bogs is the occurrence of peat mosses (*Sphagnum* mosses). Long periods of peat moss growth results in the accumulation of peat as a substrate for other plant growth. Besides living peat mosses, our peat bogs support shore pines and acid-loving shrubs.

Bogs were always rare habitats in the coastal dry belt. Virtually nothing of them remains today after some 170 years of colonial landscape modification. Vegetation elements of peat bogs are extremely rare in our area and are of particular interest to the naturalist.

Table 12 lists the principal species of dry belt peat bogs. It has been pieced together from the very few remnants of this vegetation type still found in our area and from examples in the adjacent vegetation zones.

Table 12: List of Principal Dry Belt Peat Bog Species

Trees

Pinus contorta var. *contorta* (shore pine)

Shrubs

Rhododendron groenlandicum (Labrador-tea)

Kalmia microphylla var. *occidentalis* (western bog-laurel)

Spiraea douglasii (hardhack)

Mosses

Sphagnum capillifolium (common red peat-moss)

Sphagnum fuscum (common brown peat-moss)

Sphagnum pacificum (Pacific sphagnum)

Sphagnum squarrosum (shaggy peat)

Sphagnum papillosum (fat peat-moss)

Aulacomnium palustre (glow moss)

Herb Layer and Graminoids

Rhynchospora alba (white beak-rush)

Vaccinium oxycoccos (bog cranberry)

Drosera rotundifolia (round-leaved sundew)

Lysimachia europaea ssp. *arctica* (northern starflower)

Eriophorum chamissonis var. *chamissonis* (Chamisso's cottongrass)

Carex echinata var. *echinata* (star sedge)

Carex livida (pale sedge)

Carex leptalea ssp. *pacifica* (bristle-stalked sedge)

Hypericum anagalloides (bog St. John's-wort)

Lichens

Cladina spp. (reindeer lichens)

In Canada, the three main types of wetlands are swamps (compare elements of Table 4, Table 10), marshes (compare Table 11) and bogs. While bogs cover a substantial portion of land in Canada, especially in the north, they are among the rarest of ecosystems in British Columbia's coastal dry belt.

Peat bogs, or simply *bogs*, are generally defined as wetlands whose "soils" accumulate peat derived from *Sphagnum* mosses, while *fens* accumulate the soil's organic matter from sedges, grasses and other wetland vegetation. Neither contain solid mineral matter in their soil substrates.

Fens sometimes surround peat bogs. They are not covered in this guide as they are now virtually absent in our altered landscape.

Sphagnum peat accumulates faster than other organic matter, mainly due to its strongly acidic nature, which prevents decomposition. This is why, over eons, the centres of functioning peat bogs are rising incrementally above the surrounding landscape ("raised bogs"). To the authors' knowledge, none of the remnants of our dry belt bogs retain this feature.

13-0 *Pinus contorta* **var.** *contorta* **(shore pine)** is the only tree in this plant community and is frequently the only species remaining on the sites of former peat bogs after the associated species—and in particular the *Sphagnum* mosses—have disappeared. (Note: Shore pine is familiar to us from section 8, where it is described for dry hill-country sites. However, within the dry belt landscape, this tree is equally or more common in the wet environment of bogs. To avoid confusion for the beginner working through section 8, we have assigned a new image number, 13-0, to the shore pines of bogs.)

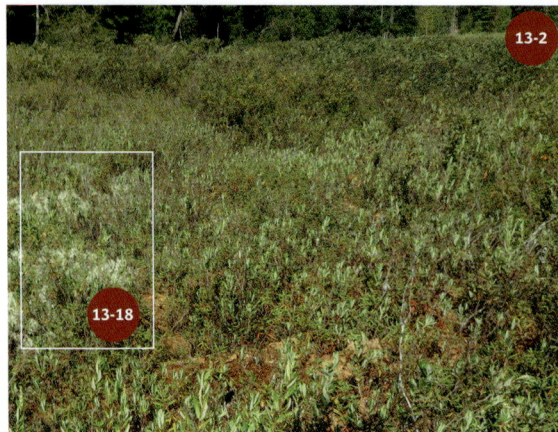

In bogs, the shrub layer is low and simple, usually consisting of **13-1 *Rhododendron groenlandicum* (Labrador-tea)** and **13-2 *Kalmia microphylla* var. *occidentalis* (western bog-laurel)**. Scattered individuals of 5-8 *Spiraea douglasii* (hardhack) are nearly always present. 1-10 *Gaultheria shallon* (salal) usually occurs in the marginal zone of the bogs under the pine trees.

Kalmia and *Rhododendron*, both in the heather family (*Ericaceae*), have characteristic leaves that can easily be distinguished in the field even when flowers are absent: 13-2 *Kalmia* leaves are dark green and glossy on the upper side and have a smooth whitish coating underneath (see left side of image 13-2a); 13-1 *Rhododendron* leaves have a wrinkly lighter green surface with a rusty to whitish coat of woolly hairs underneath, as shown in the inset photos for 13-1. In summer the leaves of both shrubs have a rolled-under leaf margin to reduce transpiration. The decoratively shaped petal cup of *Kalmia* is dropped as a whole after flowering (see right side of image 13-2a).

The following species are frequent in the herbaceous layer

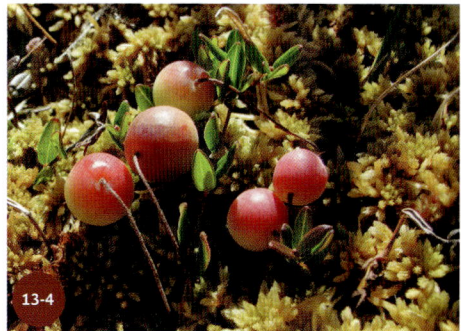

13-3 Rhynchospora alba (white beak-rush) is a rush-like plant with a white flower cluster, as the common name suggests.

13-4 Vaccinium oxycoccos (bog cranberry) is well known for culinary reasons, though the commercially available fruit is that of a closely related species (*Vaccinium macrocarpon*). As shown in our photo, the fruit can attain 10 millimetres in diameter, enormous compared to its diminutive trailing vines and leaves.

13-5 Drosera rotundifolia (round-leaved sundew) is the best-known carnivorous plant in our local flora. Small insects such as black flies are caught on the leaf blades, which have stalked sticky glands that ensnare the insect.

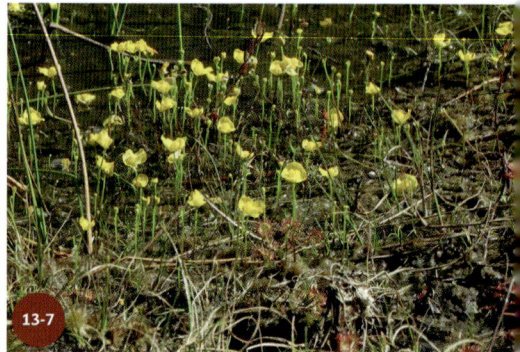

Another carnivorous plant with a quite different lifestyle is the delightfully yellow flowered **13-7 *Utricularia gibba* (humped bladderwort)**. This is a much smaller plant than 12-10 *Utricularia macrorhiza* (greater bladderwort). Both bladderworts catch small crustaceans in their tiny bladders, visible as small appendages on the submerged parts of the plant in our close-up photo of *U. macrorhiza* (12-10, section 12).

The habitats of humped bladderwort are shallow pools in peat bogs. Another small bladderwort is *Utricularia minor* (lesser bladderwort, not pictured), with narrow boat-shaped flowers. The mid-sized *U. intermedia* (flat-leaved bladderwort, not pictured) bears its bladders on special shoots.

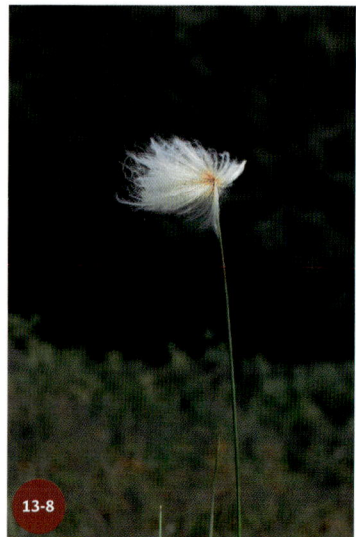

13-6 *Lysimachia europaea* ssp. *arctica* (northern starflower) is the smaller cousin of our common forest species 1-20 *Lysimachia latifolia*.

13-8 *Eriophorum chamissonis* var. *chamissonis* (Chamisso's cottongrass) bears a single plume of whitish perianth bristles on an unbranched 30-to-40-centimetre-tall stem. The upright grass-like leaves are shorter than the flowering stem.

The foliage of **13-9 *Carex livida* (pale sedge)** stands out by its light grey to glaucous colouration, and **13-11 *Carex leptalea* ssp. *pacifica* (bristle-stalked sedge)** is distinguished by thin needle-shaped leaves and stems and an inflorescence that could be mistaken for that of a small grass, as pictured in the detail photo. The common name of **13-10 *Carex echinata* var. *echinata* (star sedge)** describes the star-like fruiting cluster of this sedge.

The tiny plants of 11-23 *Hypericum anagalloides* (bog St. John's-wort), featured in section 11 (Marshes), are also found in peat bogs.

Sphagnum mosses are the defining feature of peat bogs. While microscope or at least hand lens work is needed to accurately distinguish different species of peat mosses, with some experience the combination of shape and colour can go a long way toward helping in identification.

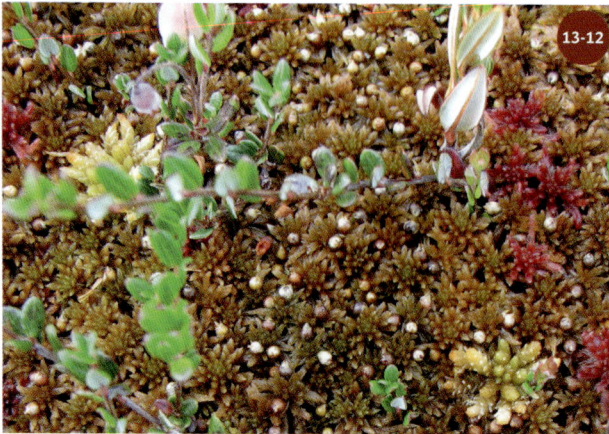

The species most easily distinguished by colour is **13-12** *Sphagnum fuscum*, which always has the same characteristic yellow-brown hue. Rather identical in size and proportions is **13-13** *Sphagnum capillifolium*. However, this species can vary considerably in colour, from reddish or pink all the way to pale green.

13-14 *Sphagnum pacificum*, normally tan to greenish, is a more robust, medium-sized species with longer branches.

Two large species are **13-15 *Sphagnum squarrosum*** and **13-16 *Sphagnum papillosum***. With its spreading (squarrose) leaf tips, *S. squarrosum* is unmistakable by shape. *Sphagnum papillosum* is large, usually tan to greenish, and has tightly shingled leaves forming somewhat blunt branch tips.

13-17 *Aulacomnium palustre* (glow moss) is a large pale green moss often associated with peat mosses in this habitat type. Along with mosses, richly branched lichens in the genus *Cladina* (**13-18 *Cladina* spp.**) often occupy substantial portions of the ground cover in peat bogs.

14 Tidal Marshes and Mudflats

How do you recognize these habitats?

In our area, tidal marshes and mudflats are usually associated with estuaries where freshwater enters the marine environment and mixes with saltwater. Differences in quantity, quality and dynamics of the freshwater influx can be considerable and influence the configuration of the tidal marsh. As a consequence, no two are alike in their vegetation. However, what they appear to have in common is plant growth that occurs in zones (or patches) where single species dominate instead of forming more complex plant communities. The presence and distribution of these zones depends on duration of saltwater inundation but also varies with the substrate, the currents, wind exposure and other factors.

The following four species tend to dominate in pure stands

- *Salicornia pacifica* (American glasswort)
- *Distichlis spicata* (alkali saltgrass)
- *Juncus balticus* (Baltic rush)
- *Carex lyngbyei* (Lyngbye's sedge)

14-1 *Salicornia pacifica* **(American glasswort)** is a member of the *Chenopodiaceae* (goosefoot family). As a genus, glassworts are distinguished by their succulent habit. This is the most frequently inundated vegetation of our tidal marshes.

14-2 *Juncus balticus* (Baltic rush) is between 20 and 30 centimetres tall and has slender stems arising from rhizomes. The stems are round in cross-section. What appears to be a continuous green stem with an inflorescence pointing sideways consists in fact of a longer stem below and a shorter bract above the inflorescence. The inflorescence is a bundle of 5 to 10 short-branched star-shaped flowers that appear black when closed. When in bloom and with open flowers, the pink stigmas and yellow anthers form an attractive contrast (inset photo).

14-3 *Carex lyngbyei* (Lyngbye's sedge) is a tall plant, similar overall to 11-4 *Carex sitchensis* (Sitka sedge), with one or two terminal male spikes and up to four female spikes below. Unlike Sitka sedge, it has conspicuous long-pointed scales on the female spikes, as shown on the detailed photo. Lyngbye's sedge is often found growing along riverbanks or channels in estuaries.

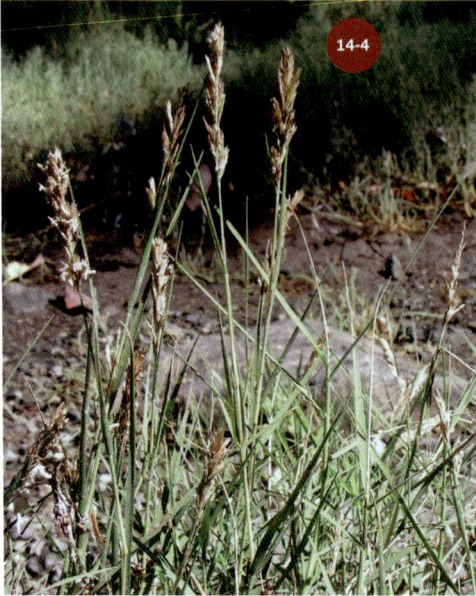

14-4 *Distichlis spicata* (alkali saltgrass) bears large, tightly grouped spikelets on short branched and leafy stems that arise from rhizomes. The relatively short grey-green leaves are sharply pointed. *Distichlis spicata* is a grass that can form dense mats, virtually to the exclusion of other species. It usually occurs in habitats that are submerged for shorter periods each day than those with 14-1 American glasswort.

Species also found in the lowest zone with American glasswort, but in much smaller numbers and often widely scattered, are **14-5 *Lysimachia maritima* (sea milkwort)** and **14-6 *Spergularia canadensis* var. *occidentalis* (Canadian sand-spurry)**, which is often replaced by the similar introduced *Spergularia marina*.

14-7 *Triglochin maritima* **(seaside arrowgrass)** and **14-8**
Puccinellia nuttalliana **(Nuttall's alkaligrass)** occur in less
frequently submerged areas.

Species that may occur scattered at the same level as 14-4 *Distichlis spicata* (alkali saltgrass) are **14-9 *Grindelia stricta* (Oregon gumweed)**, **14-10 *Plantago maritima* (sea plantain)**, **14-11 *Festuca rubra* ssp. *aucta* (Aleut red fescue)**, **14-12 *Hordeum brachyantherum* (meadow barley)**, **14-13 *Potentilla anserina* ssp. *pacifica* (Pacific silverweed)** and **14-14 *Cuscuta pacifica* var. *pacifica* (salt marsh dodder)**. The salt marsh dodder is a parasite, pictured on American glasswort (14-1). The roots of 14-13 Pacific silverweed were prepared and eaten by Indigenous peoples throughout the area (Turner & Kuhnlein, 1982).

Beach and Sand Dunes

How do you recognize these habitats?

Beach and sand dunes in the coastal dry belt occupy the area at ocean shorelines where the ground is made up of sand, gravel or fractured rock. These are mainly open habitats exposed to lots of light.

This section is a summary of native plants you can expect on beaches, sand dunes and in marine shoreline habitats other than tidal marshes and mudflats.

Dune or other beach habitats with shifting sands contain some of our most spectacular native plants. As shown in the images above, **15-1** *Abronia latifolia* **(yellow sand verbena)** often grows together with **15-2** *Polygonum paronychia* **(black knotweed)**, a small shrub.

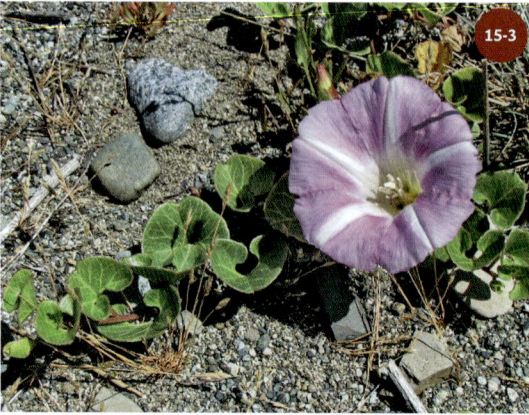

15-3 *Calystegia soldanella* (beach bindweed) has somewhat similar trailing shoots and rounded leaves to those of *Abronia*, but instead of an umbel of flowers, it bears enormous funnel-shaped single flowers.

15-4 *Carex macrocephala* (large-headed sedge) justifies its name by bearing a very large, spiky head of perigynia.

The rare **15-5 *Glehnia leiocarpa* (American glehnia)** has tiny white umbelliferous flowers that develop into large, decoratively clustered seeds.

The lovely **15-6 *Lathyrus littoralis* (silky beach pea)** is another rare species of the shifting sand. It is in the same family as the similarly named **15-7 *Lupinus littoralis* (seashore lupine).**

15-8 *Poa confinis* (beach bluegrass) is a small grass of the open sand. The rare dune beachgrass *Poa macrantha* (not pictured) is like a larger version of *Poa confinis*. Adapted to sandy substrates, both grow from extensive networks of rhizomes.

The largest and most conspicuous native grass on the seashore is **15-9 *Leymus mollis* (dune wildrye)**. Despite its common name, it is not strictly bound to the dune habitat but also grows along gravelly or shingle beaches without shifting sands.

15-10 *Artemisia campestris* ssp. *pacifica* (northern wormwood) is found on beaches and sand dunes, especially in the northern part of the dry belt.

Another member of the *Asteraceae*, **15-11 *Ambrosia chamissonis* (silver burweed)**, concludes our list of sand-dwelling native plants. It tends to form large, regularly distributed round patches when given enough space.

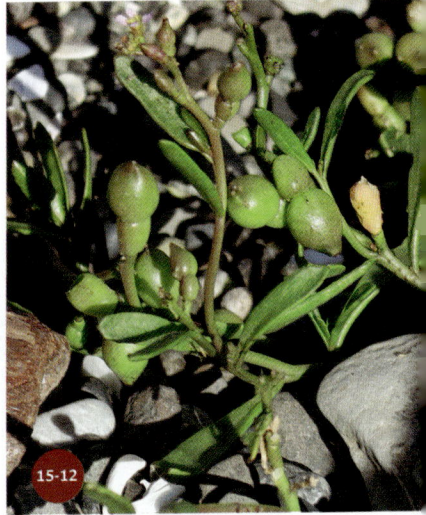

15-12 *Cakile edentula* (American searocket) is a fleshy-leaved member of the *Brassicaceae* (mustard family). It grows on gravel and sand, often among beach logs.

Several other native species are closely associated with shoreline habitats and beaches but not necessarily with sand. They are often found in coarse gravel, broken rock or even cracks in solid bedrock.

Also in the *Brassicaceae* (mustard family), **15-13** **Lepidium virginicum ssp. *menziesii* (Menzies' pepperweed)** grows in many barren places but is most common along the seashore.

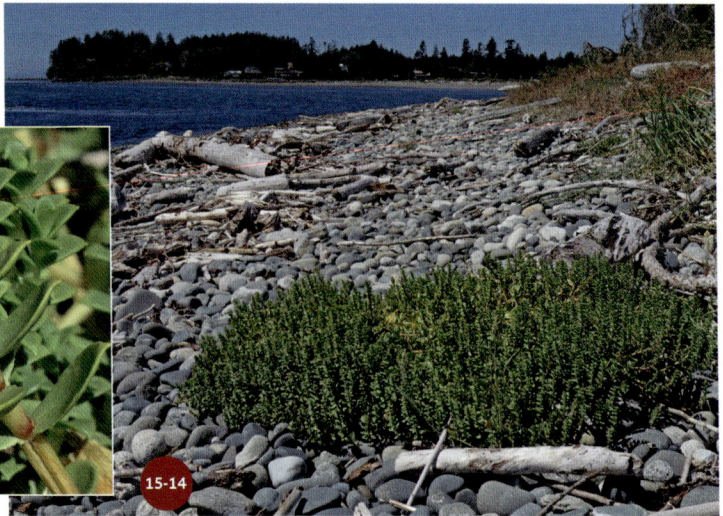

15-14 ***Honckenya peploides* (seabeach sandwort)**, like 15-12 *Cakile*, also somewhat succulent and of similar habitats but of a different architecture, belongs to the *Caryophyllaceae* (pink family).

15-15
Lathyrus japonicus
(beach pea)
is common in
sandy and other
shoreline habitats.

Several species of orache
(*Amaranthaceae* family) are
also commonly found along
beaches. **15-16 *Atriplex gmelinii***
(Gmelin's orache) is the main native
species of this genus, but it is usually
less common than the introduced
Atriplex patula. Both occupy gravelly
and sandy shorelines.

16 Shoreline Bluffs

How do you recognize these habitats?

Shoreline bluffs in the coastal dry belt are found close to tidewater. The bluffs often have a flattish top with shallow soils and jagged rocky sides. Where the soils are dry and shallow, we can see many of the same species as are found in the Garry Oak realm. The steeper, lower parts of these bluffs are influenced by salt spray and support salt-tolerant species.

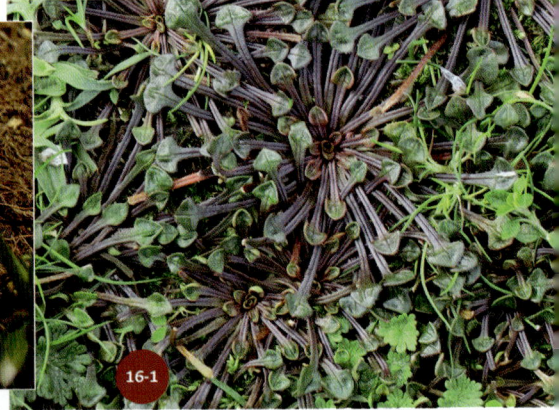

16-1

16-2

16-1 *Calandrinia ciliata* (desert rock purslane) introduces one of the first splashes of spring colour on the upper parts of shoreline bluffs. The second image under this photo identification number shows the distinctive leaves of this *Calandrinia*, often seen as early as January.

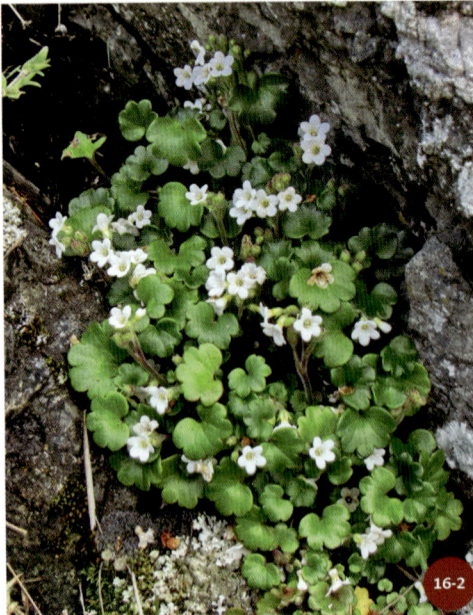

16-2 *Romanzoffia tracyi* (Tracy's romanzoffia) is another early-season gem of some coastal bluffs. With slightly succulent leaves arising from small tubers, it is always found on the shady side of the bluff.

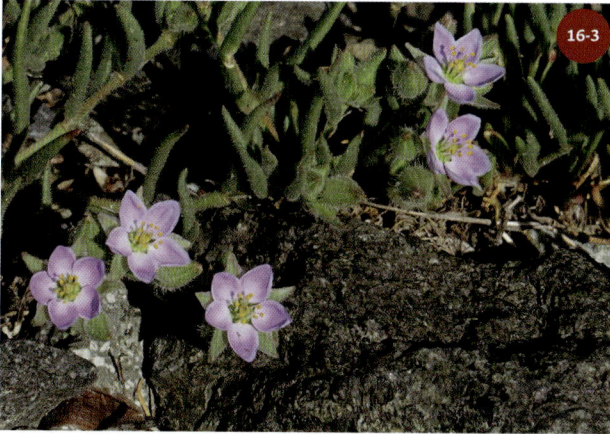

16-3 *Spergularia macrotheca* (beach sandspurry) does not strictly follow its common name, as it is more common on bedrock or broken rock than on beaches. It is the largest and showiest of this genus.

16-4 *Sedum lanceolatum* var. *nesioticum* (lance-leaved stonecrop) is a distinctive variety of stonecrop highly associated with seashore bluffs and rocky headlands.

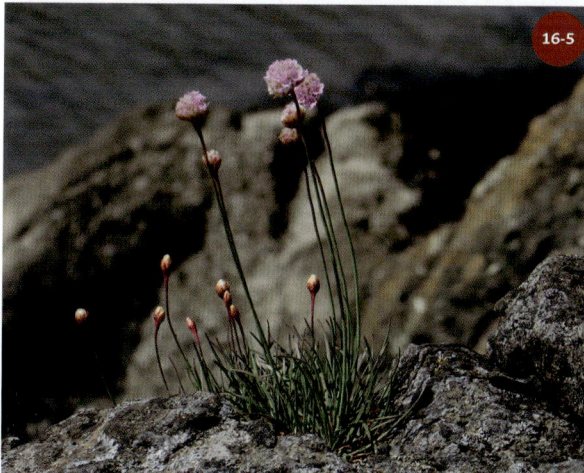

16-5 *Armeria maritima* ssp. *californica* (thrift) follows the stonecrop, blooming in June. It is at its prettiest on cliffs above the ocean but can also be found in the transition area between sandy beaches and more vegetated habitats.

Another species that is almost always present is 14-9 *Grindelia stricta* (Oregon gumweed). Here it grows in the saltspray zone, though in a less luxuriant form than in the saline mudflats (compare 14-9 on p. 154 in "Tidal Marshes and Mudflats").

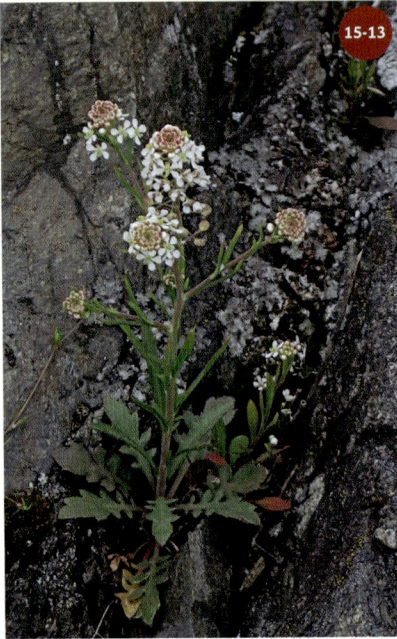

As we saw in the beach and dune habitats, 15-13 *Lepidium virginicum* ssp. *menziesii* (Menzies' pepperweed) is ever-present. It is pictured here in its spring condition.

16-6 and **16-7** show a native form of *Festuca rubra* (**red fescue**) that is common on coastal bluffs, usually growing in rock crevices. In earlier taxonomic treatments, it was designated as *Festuca rubra* ssp. *pruinosa*. The meaning of pruinosa is "frosted-over" and refers to the typical grey or glaucous colour exhibited by this form.

14-8

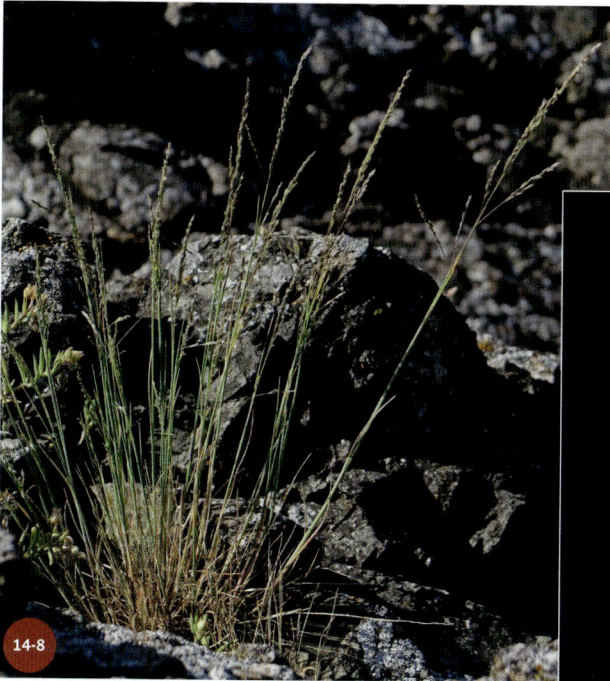

Another grass always present on the rocky saltspray-exposed parts of our shoreline bluffs is 14-8 *Puccinellia nuttalliana* (Nuttall's alkaligrass). It is familiar from lower zones of the tidal mudflats described in section 14.

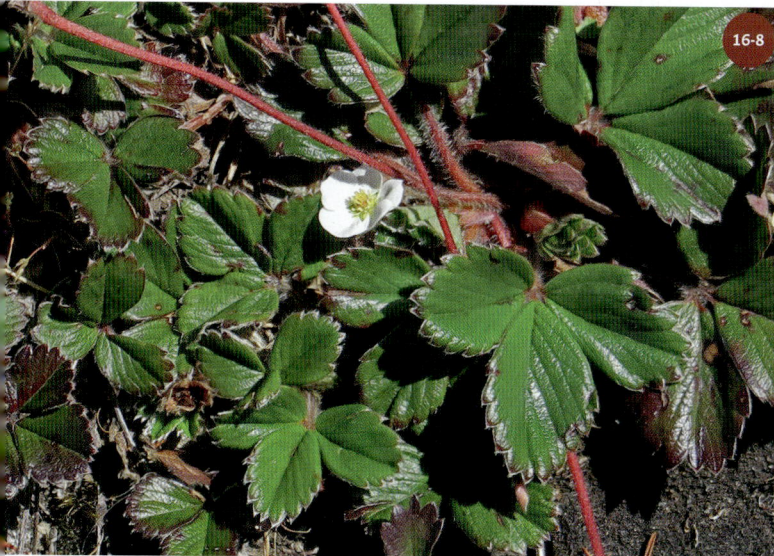

16-8

16-8
Fragaria chiloensis
ssp. *pacifica*
(coastal
strawberry)
shares this
exposed, mostly
rocky habitat
with sandy
places along the
shoreline. The
shiny, rather
tough leaves
are a prominent
feature of
this species.

Apart from sandy places, this habitat is one of the most likely in which to find **16-9 *Claytonia rubra* (redstem springbeauty)**, a tight rosette of small leaves and stems with large bracts and flowering parts, both somewhat succulent.

Most of the coastal occurrences of **16-10 *Opuntia fragilis* (brittle prickly-pear cactus)** are also on these rocky bluffs.

ADDITIONAL NATIVE PLANTS OF INTEREST

UP TO THIS POINT IN THE GUIDE WE HAVE RELIED ON EASILY RECOGNIZED plant communities or distinctive habitats to help familiarize ourselves with their species. We have listed and pictured these individual species in order of the frequency of their occurrence in those communities. Frequencies were based on extensive sampling of the communities by the senior author. While a large proportion of the native flora, including the most important species to know, has been captured in this way, many species of interest remain unaccounted for. These include, but are not restricted to, the following:

1. Native plants that are infrequent or rare in the major communities
2. Plants missed in the community sampling because they occur on micro-habitats such as rock faces
3. Plants that consistently occupy fringe or transitional habitats

Species are again grouped by their habitats, with the exception of these three:

· Trees and Shrubs
· Graminoids (grass-like plants, including grasses, sedges and rushes)
· Ferns

These last three groupings, while not habitat-based, reduce the number of species to deal with in the following habitat-based categories.

The sections in this segment of the guide are as follows

It is important to understand that species combined in any one of these groupings will not necessarily be found growing together.

Balsamorhiza deltoidea (deltoid balsamroot).

17-1 *Fraxinus latifolia* (Oregon ash) is a locally rare tree normally found in moist environments. It is distinguished from the introduced European ash by its hairy young twigs and foliage, and by its winter buds, which are grey rather than black.

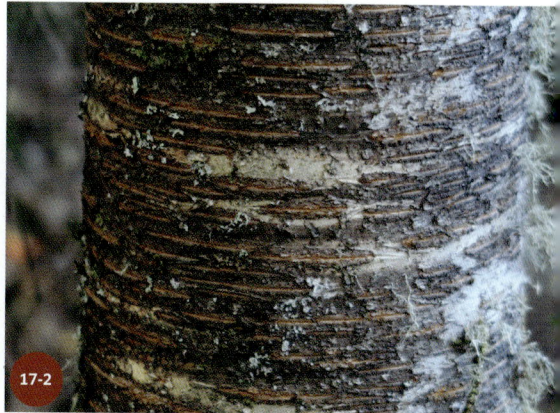

17-2 *Prunus emarginata* (bitter cherry) is a fast-growing, short-lived tree that may be found in slightly moist conifer forests. It is also known as fire cherry, apparently because it is a pioneer species that establishes itself after fires. In our contemporary landscapes, it is more common in second-growth stands than in mature forests.

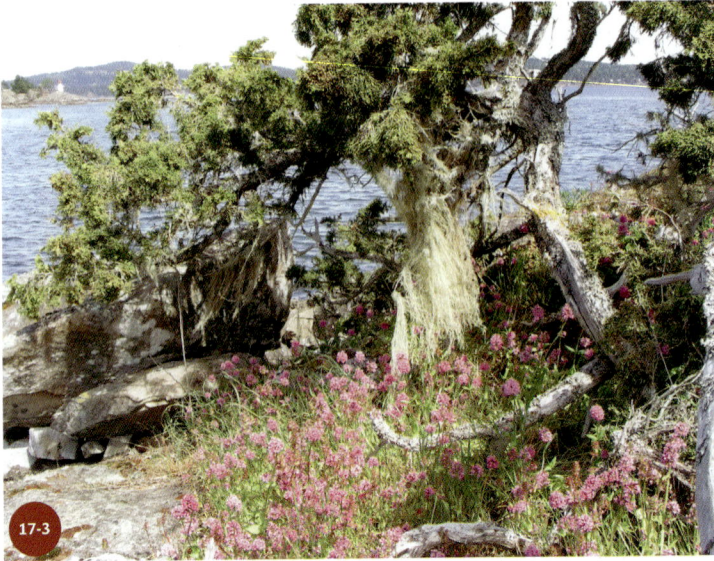

17-3 *Juniperus maritima* (seaside juniper) is often found close to saltwater, usually on exposed rocks jutting out into the water. But it also grows on ridges and hill tops further inland. The size and shape of this conifer varies greatly, from gnarly shrubs of less than 2 metres high to small, straight-stemmed cedar-like trees.

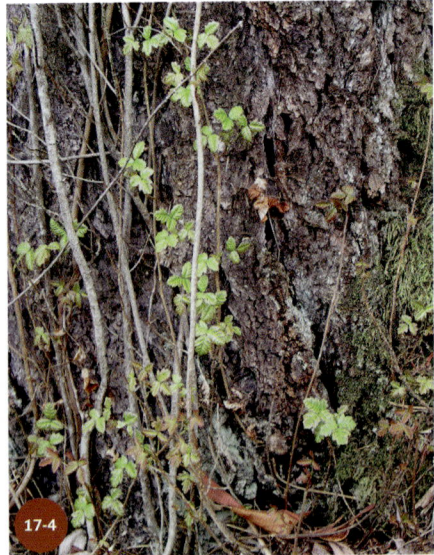

17-4 *Toxicodendron diversilobum* (poison oak) can grow as a low shrub on the forest floor but can also be found as a vine growing up tree trunks to a considerable height. A severe skin rash results from touching the twigs or foliage.

17-5 *Philadelphus lewisii* (mock-orange) is one of our most attractive shrubs, but it is difficult to define a typical habitat for it. In our area it can be found at the base of rock walls, growing in rock talus or in a variety of other, mostly treed habitats. It is heavily browsed by native black-tailed deer, and this contributes to its relative rarity and the variety of habitats it is found in.

Another attractive and frequently cultivated native shrub is **17-6 *Ribes sanguineum* (red flowering currant)**. It too can be found in a variety of habitats, from rock outcrops to wet sites.

17-7 *Sambucus cerulea* (blue elderberry) has a spotty distribution in the dry belt. It is possible that it is only present where it was introduced by Indigenous peoples.

17-8

17-8 *Vaccinium ovatum* (evergreen huckleberry) is an uncommon shrub in the dry belt, except where it can grow on sandy soils.

17-9

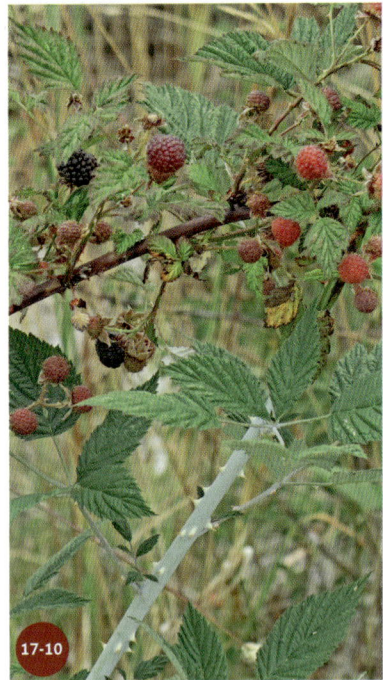

17-10

It would be difficult to name the original wild habitat for **17-9 *Ribes lobbii* (gummy gooseberry)**, which is now found mainly on recently cleared land, sometimes in large numbers. This spiny shrub has attractive flowers reminiscent of fuchsia blooms. Later in the season, it bears large fruits, but they are not very palatable.

17-10 *Rubus leucodermis* (black raspberry) is another enigma as far as its native wild habitat or plant community is concerned, as it too is now found only on logged-over land.

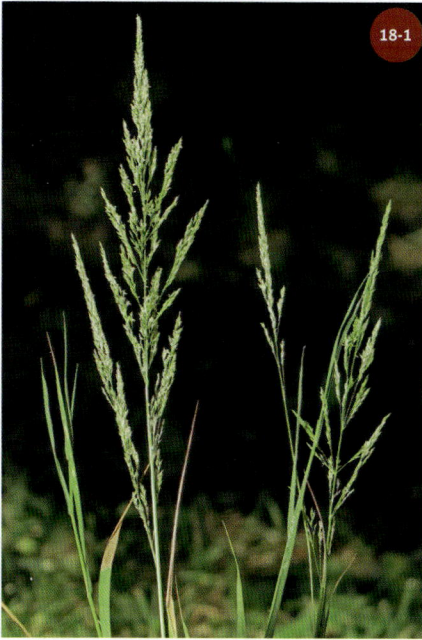

18-1 *Agrostis exarata* **(spike bentgrass)** is a ubiquitous native grass but defies association with distinct plant communities. It is found in edge or fringe situations, often where woody plant communities border on open areas, wetlands or shorelines. It is distinguished by a dense panicle of minute spikelets that cover the inflorescence branches almost down to the main stem and by relatively wide leaves with an even taper.

18-2 *Poa secunda* **ssp.** *secunda* **(Sandberg's bluegrass)** is a tufted, slender 40-to-60-centimetre grass with relatively short foliage. It is found from low-elevation Garry oak meadows to upper-elevation grasslands, either in shallow soil or rooted in cracks in the bedrock. In the past, taxonomists distinguished several other forms of the *Poa secunda* complex under their own species names. One of them, then known as Canby's bluegrass, also occurs in the Garry oak realm and is recognized by its extremely short leaves.

9-2 *Danthonia californica* (California oatgrass) has been described as one of the dominant species in Garry oak meadows and upper-elevation grasslands. Two other species of this genus, **18-3 *Danthonia intermedia* (timber oatgrass)** and **18-4 *Danthonia spicata* (poverty oatgrass)**, are found in similar dry habitats on shallow soils. Both are more common on upland terrain than at sea level. As shown in our image, *Danthonia intermedia* has shorter leaves and smaller spikelets than *D. californica*. The same applies to *Danthonia spicata*. What distinguishes the two is that the culms of *D. intermedia* spread at an angle, while those of *D. spicata* point straight up.

18-5 *Dichanthelium oligosanthes* ssp. *scribnerianum* (Scribner's witchgrass) is a low millet-like grass with broad leaves and large globular spikelets. It occurs on hot south-facing, often rocky slopes subject to early-season seepage. It is like a giant edition of the more common 9-23 *Dichanthelium acuminatum* (western witchgrass), introduced in section 9b.

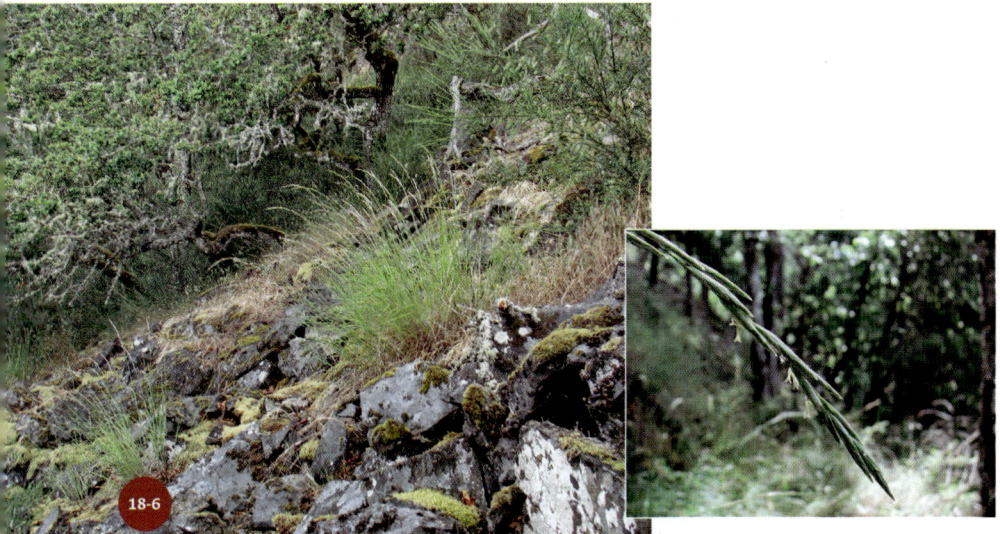

18-6 *Melica harfordii* (Harford's melic) is a relative of the much more common 1-29 *Melica subulata* (Alaska oniongrass) featured in the Douglas-fir forests of section 1. Harford's melic grows from rhizomes and occurs in loose soil or talus on steep slopes, both in shaded and open situations.

18-8 *Trisetum cernuum* (nodding trisetum) is another species found in wet forests. In contrast to its sister species, *Trisetum canescens* (2-23), which has an upright inflorescence, the flower cluster in this species is bent over and nodding, as the name suggests.

18-7 *Cinna latifolia* (nodding wood-reed) is a tall and fragile grass of moist to wet forests, only occasionally found in the coastal dry belt.

18-9 *Elymus hirsutus* (hairy wildrye) is a less common relative of 2-13 *Elymus glaucus* (blue wildrye, section 2). *E. hirsutus* typically has a bent-over, arching inflorescence and bears awns up to 10 millimetres long. It favours damp, shady habitats and is more often found in the transitional area to the next-wetter climatic zone.

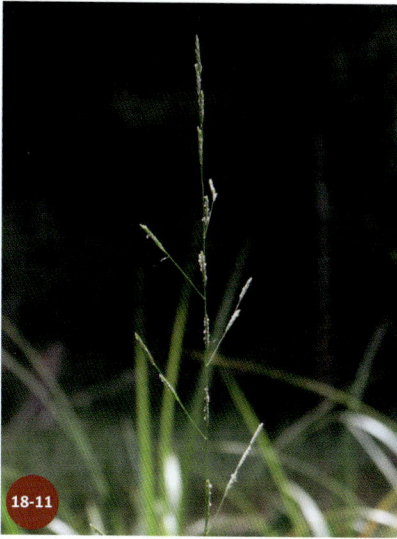

18-10 *Deschampsia cespitosa* **ssp.** *beringensis*
(tufted hairgrass) is the tall grass abundant
in estuaries and low-lying meadows. It bears
many small, awned spikelets on flexible
stems and inflorescences. An easy way to
confirm your identification of this grass
without the use of a hand lens is to hold one
of the narrow basal leaves toward the sun.
You should see several conspicuous white
lines paralleling the leaf margin.

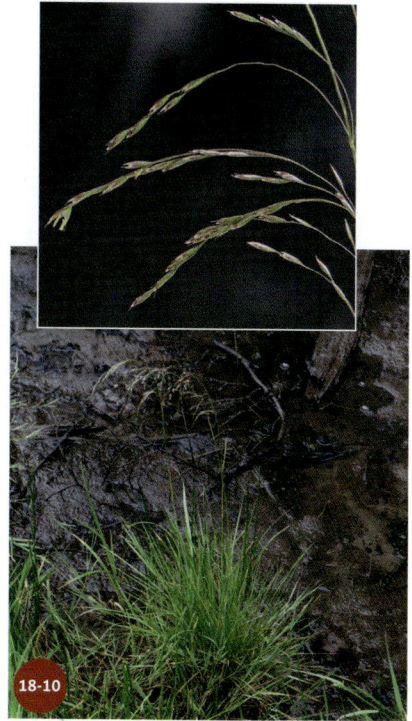

18-11 *Glyceria* × *occidentalis*
(western mannagrass) is a wetland species
that usually grows along the edge of sloughs
and ponds. It is a member of a group of five
species that all possess the same elongated
spikelets shown in our photo and that may
be encountered in the coastal dry belt. It is
assumed to be a hybrid between the native
Glyceria leptostachya and *Glyceria fluitans*, an
introduced species. Hence the "x" in front of
its specific name.

To complete the grasses, we must enter the
weedy world of the genus *Vulpia*. Here, it
is important to point out that we have
a single native member of that group,
18-12 *Vulpia microstachys* **var.** *pauciflora*
(Pacific fescue). It is an annual grass, like the
introduced species, less common but easily
recognized by its inflorescence branches, which
point away at peculiar angles.

18-13 *Bromus sitchensis* (Sitka brome) is a close relative of 7-4 *Bromus carinatus* (California brome), which we first met in the Garry oak communities. While the latter has an upright or only slightly drooping inflorescence, the inflorescence of Sitka brome is larger and strongly bent over, at least at maturity. It is found mainly along the sides of roads, trails and other fringe habitats, making its original native habitats difficult to reconstruct.

The diminutive **18-14 *Juncus bufonius* (toad rush)** is a species of vernal pool habitats (section 29). This is our smallest rush, often no larger than 3 centimetres. In contrast to most other rushes, it is an annual plant that will come up in very large numbers if the conditions are right. In addition to the native strain, there is apparently an introduced form that is hard to distinguish. In today's landscapes, *Juncus bufonius* appears on any available moist, muddy surface. Reliable native habitats are vernal pools and parts of tidal mudflats.

18-15

18-15 *Bolboschoenus maritimus* **(seacoast bulrush)** has an architecture and foliage
very similar to the common 10-8 *Scirpus microcarpus* and in fact was in the same
genus until recently. Apart from microscopic features, it is distinguished from
species in the genus *Scirpus* by having rhizomes with tubers.

18-16

18-16 *Schoenoplectus tabernaemontani*
(soft-stemmed bulrush) is the less common
species compared with 12-6 *Schoenoplectus
acutus* (hard-stemmed bulrush). As
mentioned in section 12, brackish lagoons
and regularly flooding basins on marine
clay are among its favoured habitats. While
microscopic features in the plants' floral
parts are the definitive keying distinctions
between the two species, the generally more
inflated appearance of soft-stemmed bulrush
is usually sufficient to identify this species.

18-17 *Luzula subsessilis* **(short-stalked woodrush)** is nearly as common as 7-34 *Luzula comosa* var. *laxa* (Pacific woodrush), but the Pacific woodrush is the more consistent member of undisturbed, or at least more natural, plant communities in the Garry oak realm. *Luzula subsessilis* is more often found on bare rock and on habitats disturbed by trails and trampling. The two species can be very similar at early stages of development, but mature specimens of *L. subsessilis* always have a more congested inflorescence due to shorter branches that support the flowering spikes.

18-18 *Luzula parviflora* **(small-flowered woodrush)** is a species of damp forests and is uncommon in the coastal dry belt. Both the foliage and flowering parts of this woodrush are usually gracefully bent over. This, together with small flowers, broad leaves and damp habitat, make it easy to recognize.

18-19 *Eleocharis parvula* **(small spike-rush)** is an occasional inhabitant of tidal flats, where its dwarf specimens can form a dense turf.

18-20 *Carex tumulicola*
(foothill sedge) is a tall sedge
that, upon its belated discovery
in Garry oak communities, was
believed to be extremely rare in the
province. After documentation of
more occurrences, the designation
of "imperiled" was abandoned. This
sedge may have been an important
component of Garry oak parklands
in times past, but insufficient
observations exist to confirm this.
The thin stems of this sedge are
considerably taller than the narrow
foliage, making it susceptible to
wind. Our larger image shows *Carex tumulicola*, entwined
with leaves of non-native grasses, blown to the ground.

18-21 *Carex unilateralis*
(one-sided sedge) is an uncommon but
quite distinctive sedge of vernal pool
habitats. Its inflorescence is subtended
by an extremely long bract.

18-22 *Carex feta* (green-sheathed sedge) is another
uncommon species of moist sites. Our image shows
it in a special habitat where water seeps out of a
rock crevice. Both *Carex feta* and *Carex unilateralis*
were listed as rare in earlier years.

18-23 *Carex scoparia* **(pointed broom sedge)** and **18-24** *Carex hoodii* **(Hood's sedge)** are both common species of wet meadows and often occur together.

19 Ferns

All of the seven ferns featured in this section are associated with rocky habitats, but only three (19-1, 19-2 and 19-4) are common.

19-1 *Cryptogramma acrostichoides* (parsley fern) grows on top of almost all bare or moss-covered rock outcrops.

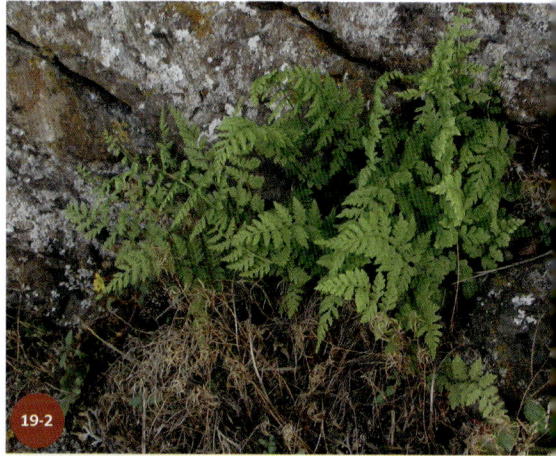

19-2 *Cystopteris fragilis* (fragile fern), while fairly common, is slightly more choosy about its micro-habitat, preferring the shelter of a rock overhang. The same is true for the pretty **19-3 *Asplenium trichomanes* (maidenhair spleenwort)**. This species is more common in wetter regional climates.

19-4 *Polystichum imbricans* (narrow-leaved sword fern) does not appear to require either shade or high humidity for survival, as it is found in full sunshine, even on south-facing slopes. It resembles sword fern except for the shorter and more abruptly tapering segments of leafy blades (pinnae) of the fern.

19-5 *Myriopteris gracillima* (lace fern) is far less common than the preceding ferns, but in the few localities where it does occur, it endures the same drought conditions as parsley fern or narrow-leaved sword fern, growing in cracks of otherwise sheer rock walls. This fern just barely enters British Columbia and is much more common in the western United States, all the way south to California.

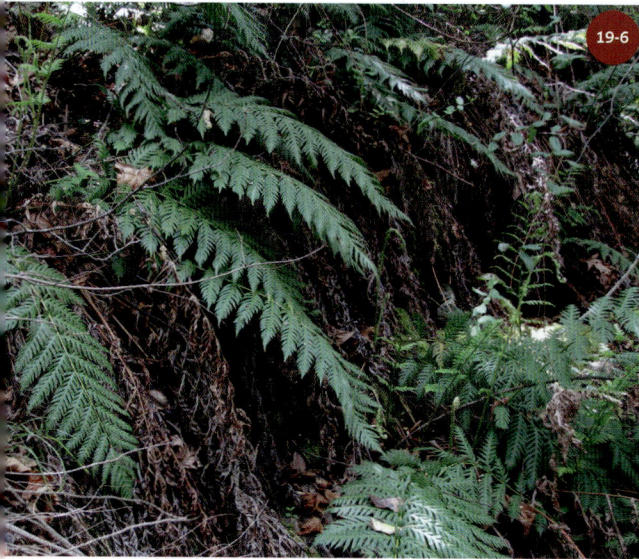

"Giant" is the key word in the common name for **19-6 *Woodwardia fimbriata* (giant chain fern)**, especially compared to the small ferns pictured here. In contrast to most of our local ferns, the dark green foliage of *Woodwardia* is evergreen. This is also a species more common further south along the coast. However, it is as rare in Washington as it is in British Columbia and only comes into its own in southern Oregon and northern California. Most of our *W. fimbriata* occurrences are in the shade of trees or on north-facing rocky sites. Some reports have occurrences of giant chain fern associated with limestone substrates. The outline of the frond is like that of a huge lady fern (4-5 *Athyrium filix-femina*), but the giant chain fern fronds are stiff and less bent over. The surface is more leathery, and the pinnules are narrowly triangular, with their widest part attached to the midrib or axis of the plant.

19-7 *Dryopteris arguta* (coastal wood fern) is a rare inhabitant of the northern Gulf Islands, where it occurs under Garry oak on south-facing sandstone cliffs. It is more common in Washington and Oregon than in British Columbia.

20 Meadows and Grasslands

This heading must be taken in the broadest sense. It includes moist and dry low-elevation and higher plant communities and those that only appear meadow-like. Species in this section should be capable of living in wide open spaces, as compared to those found in section 23, "Garry Oak and Other Dry Woodlands." As there is overlap between these habitats, it is advisable to check in both sections when identifying plants.

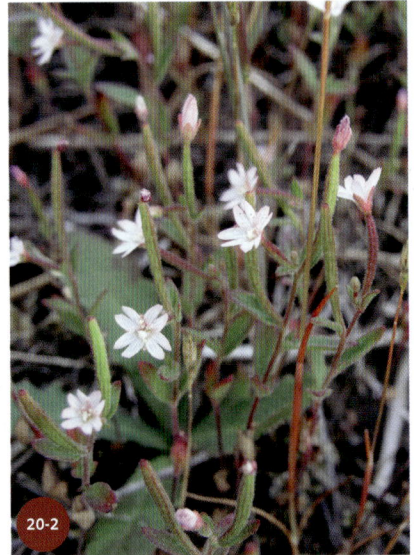

20-2 *Epilobium minutum* (small-flowered willowherb) is the small fireweed relative. It is common in the upper-level grassy areas.

20-1 *Drymocallis glandulosa* (sticky cinquefoil) is a 30-to-40-centimetre-tall perennial. Touch the stems and you will see how its glandular hairs make for the "sticky" attribute.

20-3 *Gamochaeta ustulata* (purple cudweed)
is a silver-leaved member of the aster family
(*Asteraceae*) with unassuming small flowering
parts that always seem to be in the bud stage.
The specific name *ustulata* translates as "burned
or scorched" and refers to the brownish tips of
the bracts subtending the flower heads.

20-4 *Sabulina macra* (slender sandwort) is a small annual in the pink family with white star-
shaped flowers, hair-thin stems and needle-shaped green leaves. It is locally common in our
upper-level grasslands but also occurs on nearly bare rock habitats, especially those with slight
seepage. It has a relatively narrow distribution along the coast, centred on Vancouver Island and
reaching into Washington state.

**20-5 *Sabulina rubella*
(boreal sandwort)** is a perennial of
the same size as *S. macra* but with
a multi-branched architecture and
greyish appearance. It prefers fine
dry scree or rock habitats and, while
less common locally, is distributed
over the northern hemisphere,
including higher elevations. These
distinctions aside, the two species
have led to misidentifications and
confusion, not the least because they
have had three different generic
names over the years: *Arenaria*,
Minuartia and now *Sabulina*.

**20-6 *Plagiobothrys tenellus*
(slender popcornflower)** is a rare species
found on dry south-facing slopes of hills,
mainly in the Gulf Islands.

**20-7 *Aphyllon fasciculatum*
(clustered broomrape)** is a broomrape
species that is normally yellow-flowered in
the coastal dry belt. It is widespread in the
province but rather uncommon locally.

20-8 *Viola praemorsa* (yellow montane violet) is another rarity. This violet barely enters our area from the south. Lowland populations have largely been lost, and it is now mainly found on hill slopes.

20-9 *Trifolium depauperatum* (poverty clover) is a rare small annual listed as "of special concern" in British Columbia and found in bloom before the moisture disappears from its shallow soils in April or May.

20-10 *Lupinus lepidus* (prairie lupine) is a rare plant found only in the extreme southern part of our area.

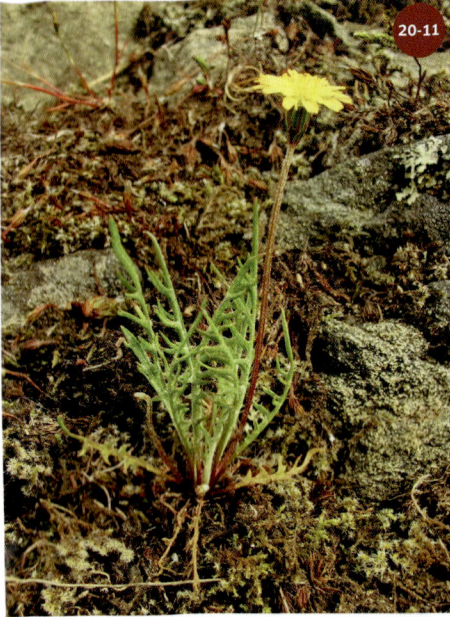

Another tiny member of the aster family is the yellow-flowered **20-11** *Microseris bigelovii* **(coast microseris)**. It is a rare species in British Columbia, Washington and Oregon. Locally, it inhabits shallow soils on coastal bluffs. As with many annuals, the size of the plants varies with available moisture, growing from less than 5 and up to 50 centimetres tall.

20-12 *Viola adunca* **(early blue violet)** sometimes occurs near the upper elevations in the coastal dry belt, but it is also common in open habitats all the way to alpine meadows.

20-13 *Silene scouleri* **(coastal Scouler's catchfly)** is known as rare all the way into Oregon. It occurs in a variety of dry meadow habitats, not far from the ocean locally, but also inland in US locations.

A minute member of the aster family, **20-14 *Crocidium multicaule* (gold star)** inhabits shallow soils, sandy islets and mossy rock areas. These small annuals sometimes occur by the hundreds and can carpet large areas in meadow-like fashion, hence its mention here.

Two additional species of broomrape are mentioned here as meadow plants. They are parasites and can also occur in a variety of other habitats, depending on their host plants.

20-15 *Aphyllon purpureum* (western one-flowered broomrape) is a common and familiar plant locally. Despite the frequency of this plant in our area, there is considerable uncertainty about its appropriate scientific name. Flora of North America has retained the generic name *Orobanche* and states that "*Orobanche uniflora* forms a polymorphic complex that requires more detailed study" (Vol. 8). The two treated subspecies are *Orobanche uniflora* subspecies *uniflora* and *Orobanche uniflora* subspecies *occidentalis*. On the basis of the length and shape of their calyx lobes, our plants would be subspecies *occidentalis*. Hitchcock and Cronquist (2018) use the name *Aphyllon purpureum* for the same taxonomic entity. In contrast, E-Flora BC name what appears to be the same plant in numerous images as *Aphyllon uniflorum* and have no entry at all for *Aphyllon purpureum*.

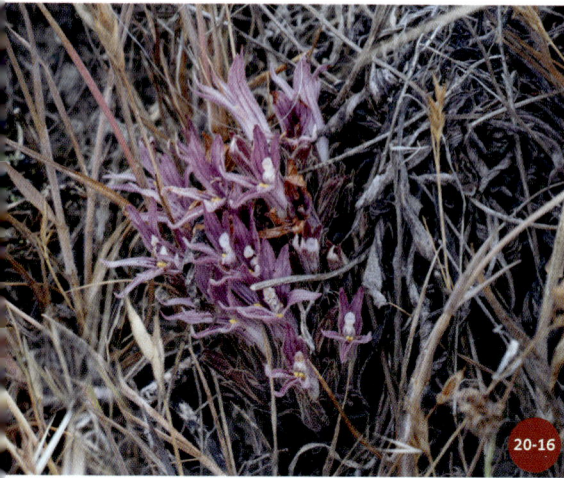

20-16 *Aphyllon californicum* ssp. *californicum* (California broomrape) is found only occasionally from shorelines to hill-country grassy habitats.

20-17 *Barbarea orthoceras* (American wintercress) typically has leaves with glossy purplish-brown highlights. Its yellow flowers are some of the earliest to show in lush meadows.

20-18 *Geranium bicknellii* (Bicknell's geranium) also likes lush meadows and sometimes a touch of seepage to thrive.

20-19 Collinsia grandiflora (large-flowered blue-eyed Mary) is easily confused with the more common 7-14 *Collinsia parviflora*, as size alone has some overlap. The inset image shows the flower's main distinctive feature, the bend of its corolla tube. The bend in the corolla tube is greater in *grandiflora* than in *parviflora*. *Collinsia grandiflora* is sparsely scattered in our area and spills over into the adjacent wetter zone.

20-20 Spiranthes romanzoffiana (hooded ladies' tresses) grows in a variety of microhabitats, from moist swales to dry meadows. It is instantly recognized by the spiral arrangement of its flowers around the stem.

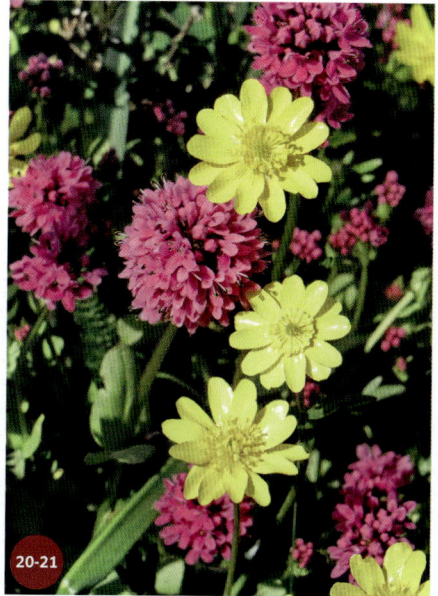

The very rare **20-21 Ranunculus californicus (California buttercup)** is distinguished from the common western buttercup (7-9) by its greater number of petals.

20-22 *Potentilla gracilis* var. *gracilis* (graceful cinquefoil) is one of many variations in this species and considered rare in the coastal dry belt, being restricted to a single locality. It occurs in lowland meadows.

20-23 *Sanicula bipinnatifida* (purple sanicle) is the rare sister species to the abundant 2-7 *Sanicula crassicaulis* (Pacific sanicle). Apart from its purple flowers, it is distinguished by more deeply cut leaves. In contrast to the common sanicle, it appears to be rare because it is eagerly sought out and consumed by deer before it has a chance to bloom and form seeds.

20-24 *Clarkia purpurea* var. *quadrivulnera* (wine-cup clarkia) is a species that comes up after a surprise rain event, when all surrounding plants have withered for their summer rest. This late appearance delayed its recognition as a member of our local flora until around 2001. This species is distinguished from the more common 9-11 *Clarkia amoena* by its reflexed sepals when in bloom and by its longitudinally ridged seed capsule. The comparative images of *Clarkia purpurea* var. *quadrivulnera* and *Clarkia amoena* show turned down (reflexed) sepals in 20-24 and turned up sepals in 9-11. The seed capsules are also different, with those of 20-24 longitudinally ridged and those of 9-11 smooth.

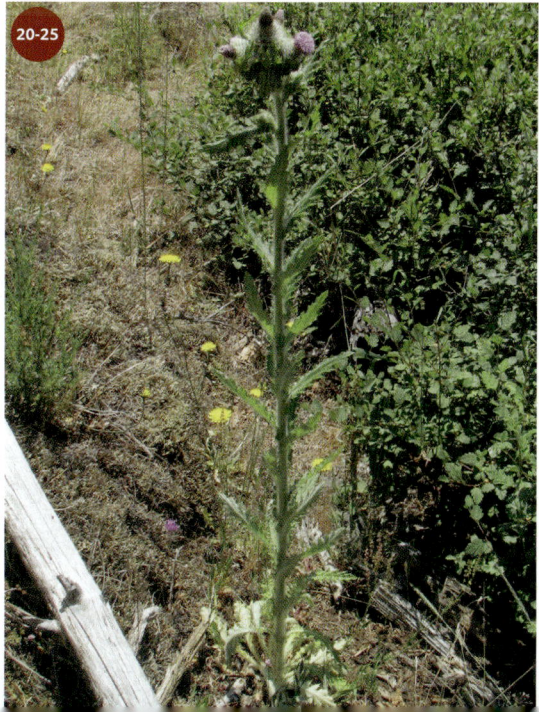

20-25 *Cirsium brevistylum* (short-styled thistle), a native species, is included in this section for want of a more suitable place, as its native habitat is difficult to determine. It inhabits disturbed vegetation types similar to those where introduced weedy thistles reside. With larger flower heads than *Cirsium arvense* (Canada thistle) and less spines than *Cirsium vulgare* (bull thistle), *Cirsium brevistylum* is easily distinguished.

21 Bare and Mossy Rock Habitats

Before we go to woodlands, we need to pay attention to species found on rock habitats and shallow soils. Some of these species are also partial to rocky habitats that are enhanced by seeps of water, especially in the spring. Seep habitats will be covered in the next section. Often there is no clear boundary between these two micro-habitats. For example, several species in the *Montiaceae* family straddle the boundary between these related sections by possessing succulent leaves.

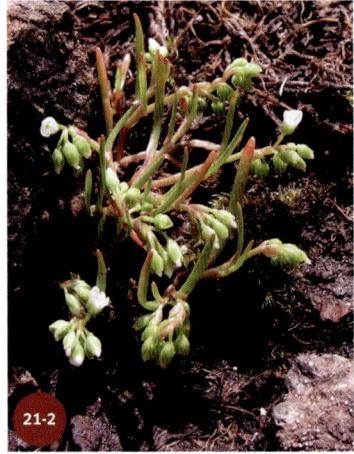

Relatively speaking, **21-1 *Montia linearis* (narrow-leaved montia)** is the largest of these mostly diminutive species. Its flowers are larger and appear singly, as compared to **21-2 *Montia dichotoma* (dwarf montia)**, which has smaller, bunched flowers.

21-3 *Claytonia exigua* (pale springbeauty) also has small, bunched flowers subtended by distinctive twin bracts. This species is further distinguished by having a peculiar whitish to blueish surface colouration and grows on open or partly shaded mossy rocks.

21-4 *Lithophragma glabrum* **(smooth fringecup)** is a member of the *Saxifragaceae* and bears small bulbils in the upper leaf axils (enlarged in the right photo). The attribute *glabrum* (smooth) seems to apply only to the basal leaves, as the rest of the plant is quite hairy.

21-5
Thysanocarpus
curvipes
(sand lacepod) is
an annual in the
mustard family
that sprouts early
in the spring, has
inconspicuous
flowers, but
later on forms
decorative
seed pods.

21-6 *Athysanus pusillus*
(common sandweed)
is yet another tiny
annual, also in the
mustard family, that is
more conspicuous for
its seed pods than its
minute flowers.

21-7 Erythranthe nasuta (little yellow monkeyflower) is an often overlooked, less common species, intermediate in size between 7-41 *Erythranthe alsinoides* and 9-21 *Erythranthe microphylla* (or 28-4 *Erythranthe guttata*, yellow monkeyflower, *E. microphylla*'s perennial look-alike; see section 28).

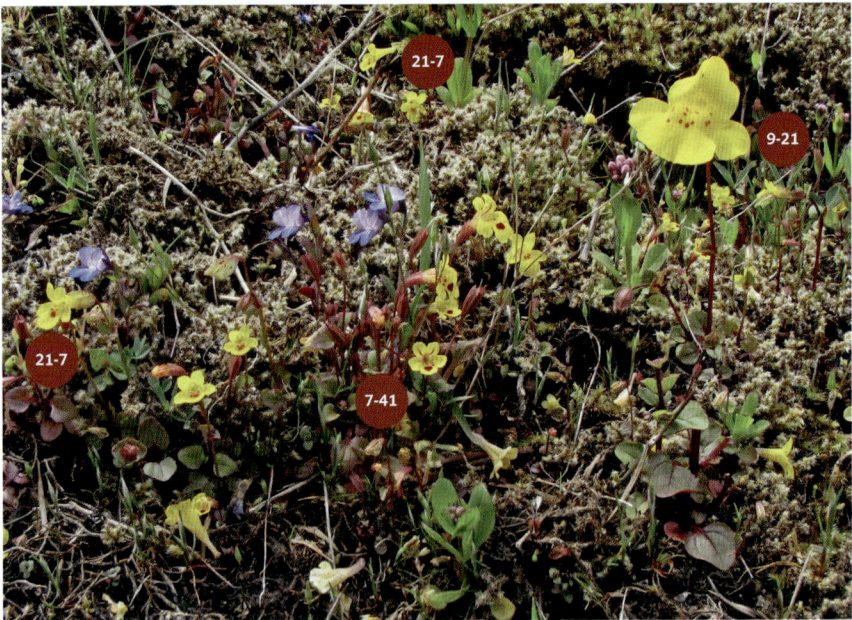

The image above allows us to compare the size and morphology of three *Erythranthe* species. Here we have a single large flower of 9-21 *Erythranthe microphylla* (small-leaved monkeyflower), the small flowers of 7-41 *Erythranthe alsinoides* (chickweed monkeyflower) arising from a narrow reddish calyx, and the intermediate-size flowers of 21-7 *Erythranthe nasuta* (little yellow monkeyflower). Flowers of the latter are seen on the left side, near the top and otherwise scattered throughout the image. They are distinguishable from *E. alsinoides* by their pale calyx.

21-8 *Erythranthe sookensis* **(shy monkeyflower)**. With a specific name honouring a community on the edge of the coastal dry belt, we cannot ignore this species. But there is a problem identifying it. According to G.L. Nesom, grandmaster of monkeyflower taxonomy, it is indistinguishable morphologically from 21-7 *Erythranthe nasuta* (Nesom, 2013). Genetic analysis is necessary to prove its identity. True, it tends to have more pronounced reddish spots on its calyx and a fruit normally exceeding the calyx, compared to the features typical for *E. nasuta*, but variation in these features in both species make for a complete overlap between the two.

The following three species are perennials in the saxifrage family. All of them seem to grow best where early-season seepage is available and could equally well be treated under the next section.

21-9 *Micranthes rufidula* **(rusty-haired saxifrage)** is deeply rooted in the cracks of rocks, often vertical or on steep inclines. It is one of the earliest spring flowers locally. The rusty hairs referred to in the common name are crowded on the underside of the leaves. The leaves are glossy green above and seem almost succulent.

The leaf rosettes and most of the plant of **21-10 *Micranthes ferruginea* (Alaska saxifrage)** are hairy and of a reddish colouration. This plant can flower as a small seedling (left photo) or as an intricately branched specimen 20 or 30 centimetres tall. This variation in plant sizes appears to be typical for the species.

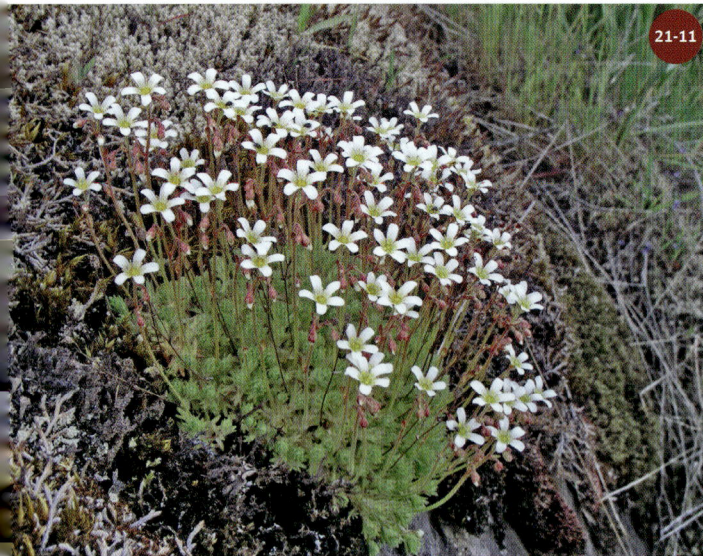

21-11 *Saxifraga cespitosa* (tufted saxifrage) is of a quite different architecture. It has many separate shoots, each ending in a small rosette of lobed leaves that bears the flowering stem. The distribution of this species reaches all the way into the alpine zone. Locally, its habitat tends to be on steep north-facing slopes and cliffs, especially where extra moisture is available.

Early Season Seepage Sites

These are habitats that collect and conduct seepage water early on but gradually dry out as precipitation decreases in late spring or early summer.

22-1 *Montia fontana* **(blinks)** is a tiny plant that is always present in seepage habitats. It often forms large wet mats in such sites. The less common **22-2** *Montia howellii* **(Howell's montia)** also thrives in these sites.

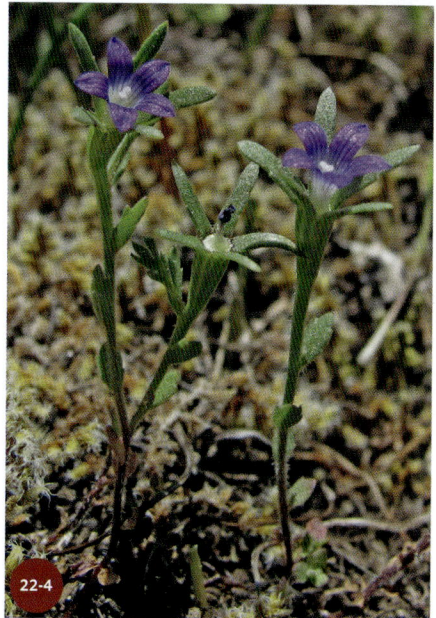

22-3 *Idahoa scapigera* **(scalepod)** forms disc-shaped seed pods on hair-thin stems arising from a minute rosette of spoon-shaped leaves.

22-4 *Githopsis specularioides* **(common bluecup)** is a rare species despite its common name denominator. It occupies sites in which slight seepage influence continues into early summer.

22-5 *Meconella oregana* (white meconella) is a minute member of the poppy family that comes into bloom in early March. It is another one of many rarities in the coastal dry belt.

22-6 *Nuttallanthus texanus* (Texas toadflax) is another rarity. It grows in draws in the pocket grasslands, where moisture lasts slightly longer.

22-7 *Trifolium wormskioldii* (springbank clover) is appended here for want of a class of its own. It is a poor fit for this habitat, being a larger plant that requires deeper soils. Indigenous peoples have traditionally eaten the rhizomes of this species (Turner and Kuhnlein, 1982).

23 Garry Oak and Other Dry Woodlands

These are habitats that include trees but are not closed forests. As mentioned earlier, some meadow plants could be listed in this category. And, by the same token, some woodland plants could be interpreted as meadow plants if they grow in woodland openings.

It is appropriate to begin with one of the most spectacular of our native wildflowers, **23-1 *Balsamorhiza deltoidea* (deltoid balsamroot)**. The reason this high-profile member of Garry oak ecosystems has not been listed earlier is because it is not a standard component of Garry oak communities but a rare species in British Columbia.

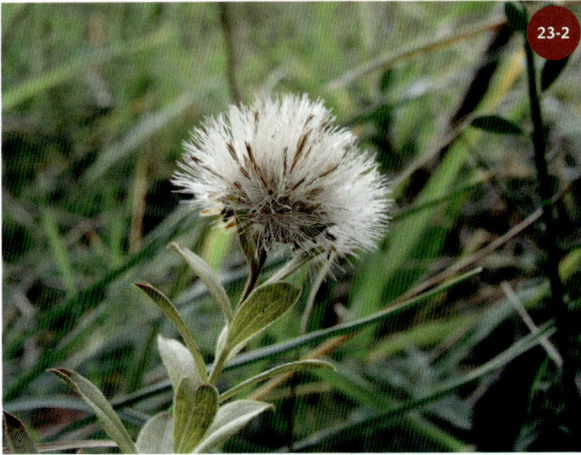

A much less showy but also rare plant of Garry oak woodlands is **23-2 *Sericocarpus rigidus* (white-top aster)**. A peculiarity of this species is that its foliage arises very early in the spring, but the plant doesn't come into bloom until early fall. The plants lack the petal-like ray florets normally found in the aster family. Instead, as shown in our photo, it possesses multiple hair-like pappus threads.

23-3 *Triteleia howellii* (Howell's triteleia) is another rare species in Garry oak communities. It belongs to the same family as camas (*Asparagaceae*, formerly *Liliaceae*) and forms tall stems with large pale blue flowers.

23-4 *Eurybia radulina* (rough-leaved aster) is yet another rarity. In some habitats it is hard, if not impossible, to find this species in flower, as it is under severe grazing pressure by deer. In fact, the first discovery of the species locally was not confirmed until after a plant was brought to flower in a garden setting.

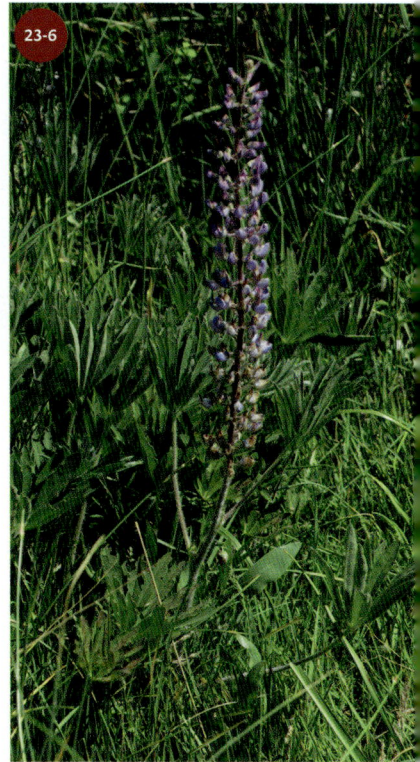

23-5 *Rupertia physodes* (California tea) is a large, almost shrub-like legume sometimes found in Garry oak woodlands. **23-6 *Lupinus polyphyllus* var. *polyphyllus* (large-leaved lupine)** is another large plant in the same family that may be found in the southern parts of the dry belt.

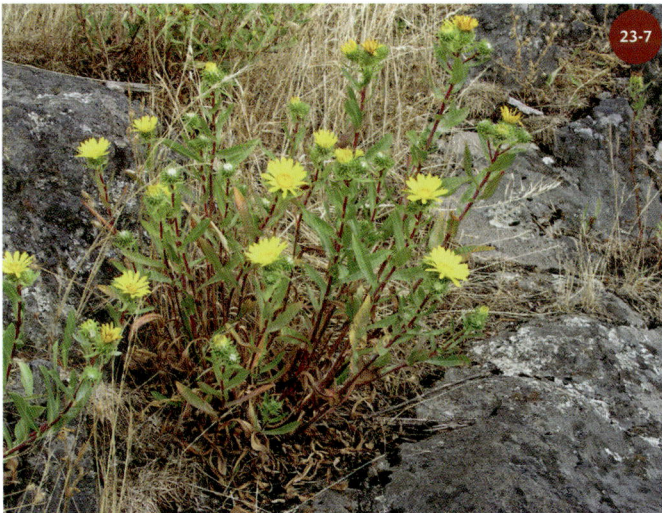

23-7 *Grindelia hirsutula* (hairy gumweed) may be found in the rocky parts of Garry oak woodlands.

23-8 *Platanthera elegans* (elegant rein orchid) is an occasional member of this habitat. It is conspicuous in early spring, when its broad leaves emerge, and in summer, when it bears its spike of white flowers. At flowering time, the leaves have usually dried away or are only shrivelled brown remnants.

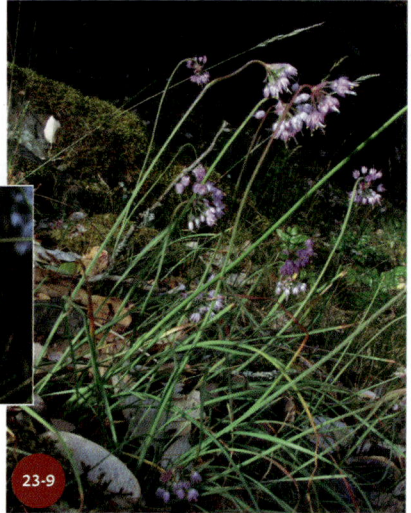

23-9 *Allium cernuum* (nodding onion) doesn't occur with enough frequency to make it into any of our dry belt tables. Instead, it is scattered in many semi-open habitats in other climatic zones, both wetter and drier. It was another important food item for Indigenous peoples.

In our area, **23-10 *Packera macounii* (Macoun's groundsel)** is only found in shore pine–Douglas-fir–arbutus woodlands (our section 8) and was considered rare until more occurrences were found. It has the white-frosted leaves typical of the genus.

23-11 *Viola howellii* (Howell's violet) is a rare plant in local woodlands. Known populations disappear several years after being reported, and this short lifespan seems to be a reason for its "rare" status.

23-12 *Ranunculus orthorhynchus* (straight-beaked buttercup) is a less common species than the ubiquitous 7-9 *Ranunculus occidentalis*. As indicated in the common name, it is distinguished by straight beaks on its seed head (compare inset images: 7-9 *R. occidentalis* left, 23-12 *R. orthorhynchus* right). In addition, leaf segments on 23-12 tend to be narrower than on 7-9.

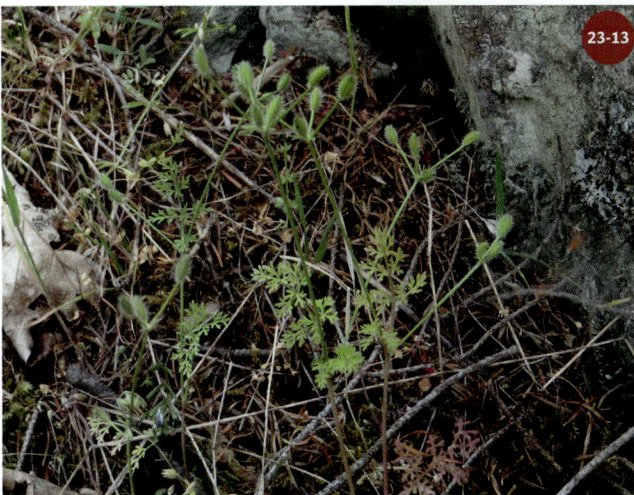

23-13 *Yabea microcarpa* (California hedge-parsley) is a member of the *Apiaceae* (in the past, more descriptively called *Umbelliferae*) family and bears the bristly seeds that are typical for many species in this family. The bristles attach to the fur of passing animals for dispersal.

23-14 *Cardamine nuttallii* (slender toothwort), a member of the mustard family (*Brassicaceae*), is an attractive wildflower in mixed woodlands. The common name appears to refer to the small tooth-like tubers that are part of the rhizomes.

23-15 *Claytonia parviflora* (streambank springbeauty) has linear basal leaves, distinguishing it from the broadly diamond-shaped ones of 7-7 *Claytonia perfoliata* (miner's-lettuce). *C. parviflora* is also found in conifer forests (our next two sections) and is less common locally.

24   Well-drained Forests

A number of species not covered in the community-based parts of this guide occur occasionally in closed, mainly conifer forests. Most are not confined to the dry belt but also occur in adjacent wetter forest zones.

The first four species shown below are known as heterotrophs. These are plants that have no green leaves and derive their nutrition from sources other than photosynthesis, through parasitism either on green plants or on fungi.

Plants that parasitize fungi are known as mycoheterotrophs. Some of these may be connected to fungal mycelia that are themselves connected to trees. Species that have leaves and perform photosynthesis but are additionally connected to fungi are called partial mycoheterotrophs (Pojar, MacKinnon, et al., forthcoming), (MacKinnon & Luther, 2021).

24-1 *Kopsiopsis hookeri* (Vancouver ground cone) is parasitic on 1-10 *Gaultheria shallon* (salal). It is a scaly cone-shaped plant that may be purplish red or yellow at flowering time. It will eventually turn black.

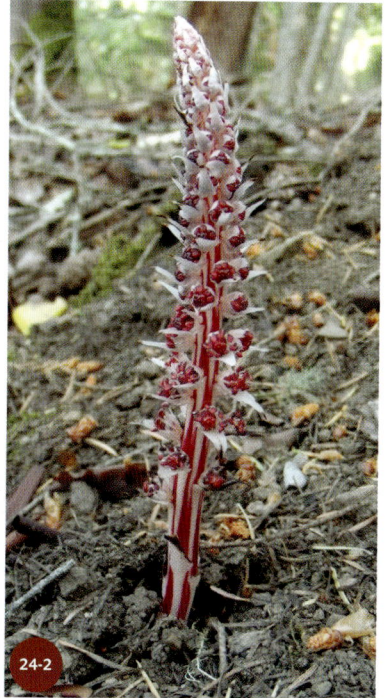

24-2 *Allotropa virgata* (candystick) is bright red and white when in bloom. It too will turn black after flowering, as do all heterotrophs except those that also have leaves.

24-3

24-3 *Pterospora andromedea* (pinedrops) is a tall plant, growing up to 1 metre high, with brownish-purple flowering parts.

24-4

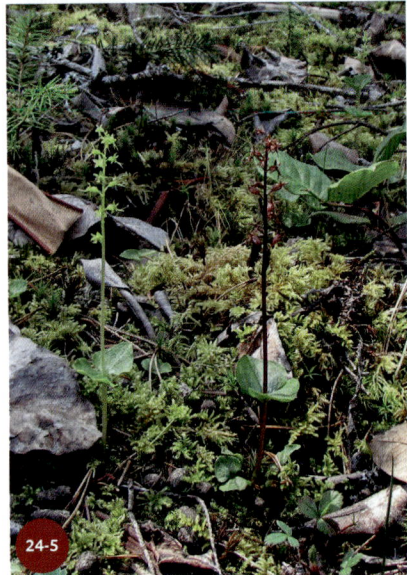

24-5

24-4 *Cephalanthera austiniae* (phantom orchid), dependent on connection to fungal mycelia, is a rare plant locally. This type of fungal connection also applies to one of our smallest orchids, **24-5 *Neottia cordata* (heart-leaved twayblade)**, which may be categorized as a partial mycoheterotroph. While light conditions don't determine the growing sites of phantom orchids, they do matter for heart-leaved twayblade, as it has small green leaves.

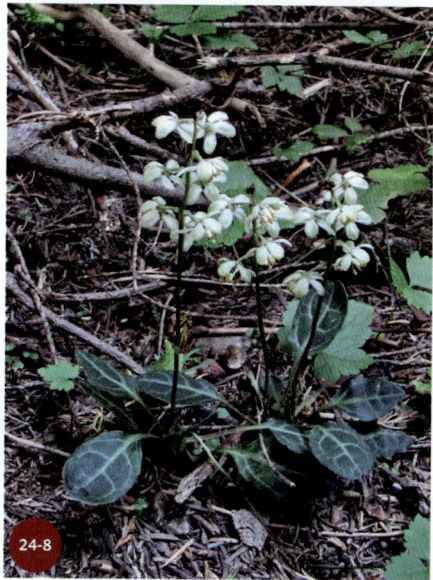

Other partial mycoheterotrophs are **24-6 *Chimaphila umbellata* (common pipsissewa)**, **24-7 *Pyrola asarifolia* ssp. *asarifolia* (pink wintergreen)** and **24-8 *Pyrola picta* (white-veined wintergreen)**.

This leaves only a few "regular" green plants in this category

24-9 Anemone lyallii (Lyall's anemone) is a dainty white-flowered forest dweller, not found everywhere, but where it shows up, it can form good-sized patches.

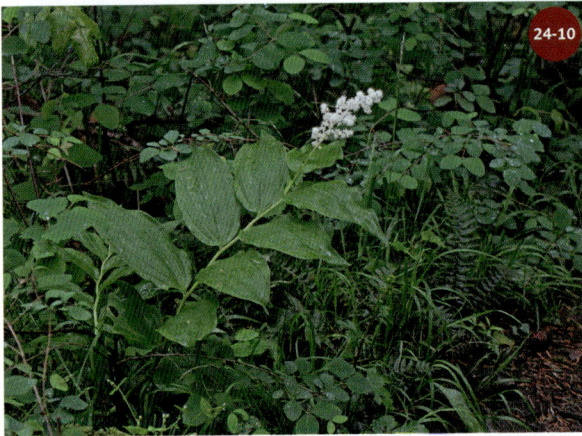

24-10 Maianthemum racemosum (false Solomon's seal) is a white-flowered member of the lily family. It can be up to 50 centimetres tall and usually grows as a single plant or in a small group. The individual flowers are quite small but, as they occur in a large, dense panicle, make for quite a showy appearance.

24-11 Maianthemum stellatum (star-flowered false Solomon's seal) has slightly larger individual flowers but in a much fewer-flowered panicle. The plants are only half the size of *M. racemosum* but, as they are connected by rhizomes, often form large colonies.

25 Moist to Wet Forests and Their Openings

With names like *alpina* and *pacifica*, one wonders where **25-1 *Circaea alpina* ssp. *pacifica* (enchanter's-nightshade)** belongs! The names are a hint to this plant's distribution. It is widespread, reaching from Alaska down almost to California and from sea level to near alpine elevations. It is a member of the evening primrose family (*Onagraceae*) and has tiny white flowers and heart-shaped to rhombic leaves.

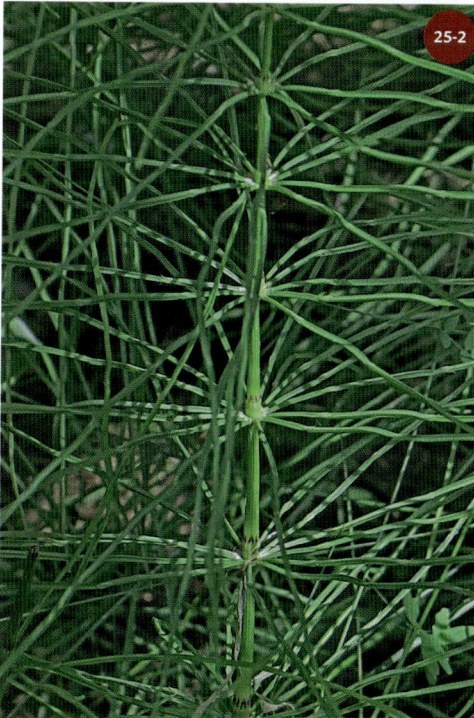

25-2 *Equisetum arvense* (common horsetail) may be the common species further inland but not here, where giant horsetail (4-8 *Equisetum telmateia*) reigns. Common horsetail is a much smaller, slimmer version of giant horsetail. In the dry belt, it occurs on the edges of wet forests, including the black cottonwood community, as well as on disturbed ground. The even less common *Equisetum palustre* (not pictured) is a look-alike.

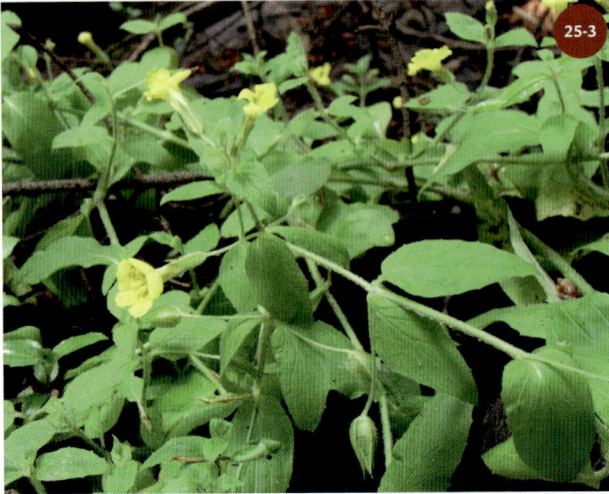

25-3 Erythranthe moschata (musk-flower) is an uncommon but attractive species in some wet forests.

25-4 Tiarella trifoliata var. laciniata (cut-leaved foamflower) has more deeply incised, narrowly lobed basal leaves but is otherwise identical to the more frequently occurring three-leaved foamflower (3-5 *Tiarella trifoliata* var. *trifoliata*). Cut-leaved foamflower is uncommon in our area and more often found further west.

26 Estuaries and Associated Wet Meadows

26-1

26-2

We featured the main saltmarsh succulent, American glasswort (14-1 *Salicornia pacifica*), in section 14 "Tidal Marshes and Mudflats." Here we turn our attention to **26-1 *Salicornia depressa* (maritime glasswort)**, a smaller infrequent plant in the same habitat. Another of these less common succulents, this one with attractive composite (aster family) flowers, is **26-2 *Jaumea carnosa* (fleshy jaumea)**.

The following three species inhabit back-shore meadows that are still influenced by saltwater but occur in the transition zone to freshwater habitats.

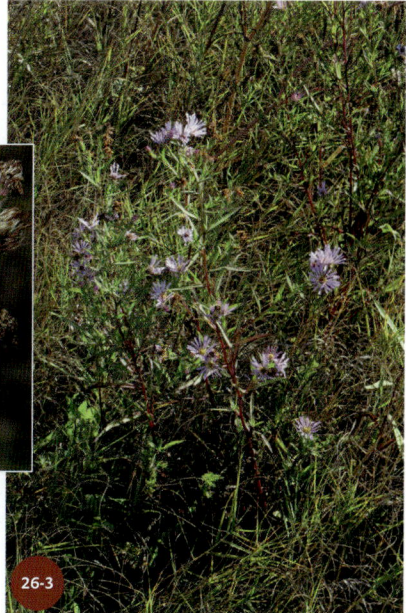

26-3

Species in this genus are notoriously difficult to identify, but **26-3 *Symphyotrichum subspicatum* (Douglas aster)** can consistently be found in this specialized habitat.

26-4 *Sidalcea hendersonii* (Henderson's checker-mallow) provides a splash of colour in this environment. It is considered rare locally.

26-5 *Rumex occidentalis* (western dock) also occupies these part-saline meadows.

27 Other Shoreline Habitats

Most of the species in this section are rare or very rare. They can be found in a variety of shoreline habitats in the coastal dry belt. However, few habitats have more than one or two of these species growing together.

The first five species are all known for their rarity.

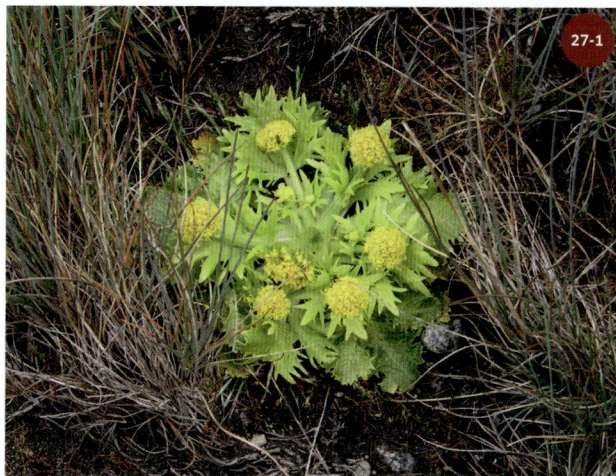

27-1 *Sanicula arctopoides* **(bear's-foot sanicle)** grows on wind-exposed and often flat shoreline bluffs, where the grass cover is short or absent. Despite its rarity, this is a conspicuous plant when it emerges with its bright yellow foliage and flowers in early spring.

27-2 *Hosackia gracilis* **(seaside bird's foot lotus)** occupies a narrow band on the edge of shoreline rocks between taller or shrubby vegetation and the drop-off. Some of these places seem to be enhanced by slight seepage from above. The flowers are attractive with their contrast between bright pink and yellow.

Clay banks facing the sea, sometimes eroding, provide the habitat for **27-3 Lupinus microcarpus var. microcarpus (dense-flowered lupine)**. Its cotyledons are remarkable in their succulence.

27-5 Camissonia contorta (contorted-pod evening-primrose) is a small sand-dweller, usually found near the base of dunes that are actively turned over by the wind.

Rock or earth embankments of a similar nature are the home for **27-4 Allium geyeri (Geyer's onion)**. This uncommon white- or pale pink-flowered onion is distinguished by bearing bulbils at the base of the flowering umbel.

27-6 *Artemisia suksdorfii* (**Suksdorf's mugwort**) is a large plant, usually clumped and up to a metre in height. It occurs along sandy or gravelly shores but can also be found on roadsides and other disturbed places.

27-7 *Oxybasis rubra* (**red goosefoot**) is also found on beaches but much closer to wave action. It is just one of many plants in the amaranth family (*Amaranthaceae*) that grow near saltwater.

27-8 *Vicia nigricans* var. *gigantea* (**giant vetch**) prefers bushy shorelines and needs woody plants to support its long tendril-equipped shoots. This species is not restricted to the dry belt but can also be found on the wet West Coast, from Alaska down to northern California.

28 Various Wet Sites

The following species also occur in wet places but do not fit any of our preceding categories.

28-1 *Cicuta douglasii* (Douglas' water-hemlock) is found in wet meadows surrounding bogs, ponds and lakes. It is one of the most poisonous plants in the local flora.

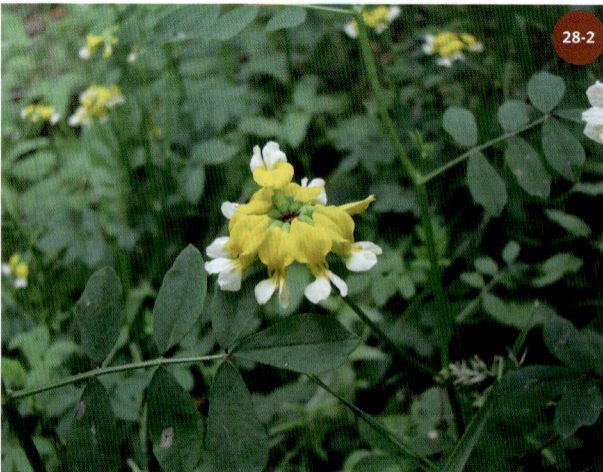

28-2 *Hosackia pinnata* (bog bird's-foot trefoil) is every bit as pretty and rare as 27-2 *Hosackia gracilis*, mentioned earlier. *H. pinnata* is a larger plant, and the white-plus-yellow flowers are arranged in an umbel. It grows in spring ponds that collect water from large rock surfaces.

28-3
***Ranunculus alismifolius*
(water-plantain
buttercup)** is another
rare species known only
from two localities in
our area. It occurs in
shallow water of wet
meadows and has an
unlobed pointed leaf.
The plants grow to
30 centimetres or larger.

When the same size,
**28-4 *Erythranthe guttata*
(yellow monkeyflower)** is
virtually indistinguishable
from 9-21 *Erythranthe
microphylla* (small-leaved
monkeyflower), except
that *E. guttata* is a
perennial rather than an
annual. However, it grows
into larger plants where
conditions allow. Pictured
here on a shoreline rock
wall, it can also be found
on gravelly river beds or
along lowland streams.

29 Vernal Pool Habitats

Vernal pools are shallow depressions that fill with water in spring but dry out later in the growing season. Sometimes they are connected to seeps and support plants that occupy the transitional habitat between the two.

Given the extremely specialized and ephemeral nature of this habitat, an astounding number of uncommon plants fit in this category. Some are high-profile rare plants locally.

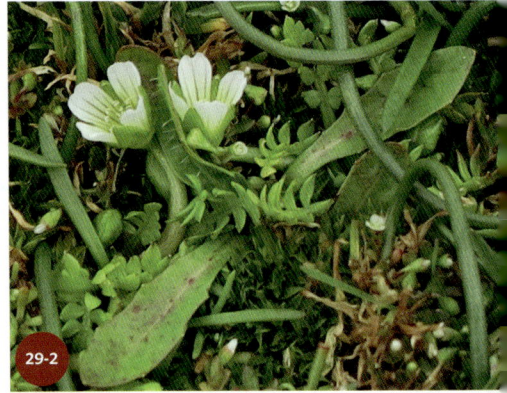

29-1 *Isoetes nuttallii* (**Nuttall's quillwort**) is a spore-bearing plant more related to ferns than to flowering plants. Its simple needle-like leaves are arranged in a star shape. The spores are produced in pockets at the base of its leaves.

The rare **29-2** *Limnanthes macounii* (**Macoun's meadowfoam**) is a small white-flowered plant with pinnate leaves.

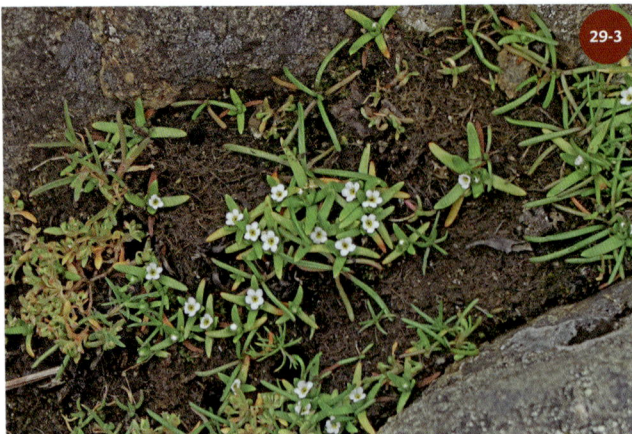

29-3 *Plagiobothrys scouleri* (**Scouler's popcornflower**) is a tiny plant with undivided leaves and white flowers. It often populates vernal pools in large numbers.

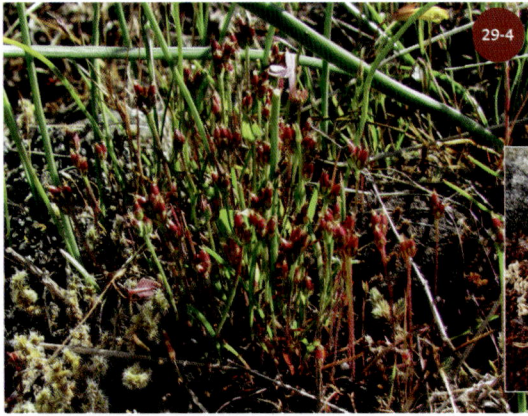

29-4 *Plantago elongata* (slender plantain) is another dwarf that can form mats of hundreds of plants in a small patch.

29-5 *Psilocarphus elatior* (tall woolly-heads) is a small member of the aster family. Its flowering and seed-bearing parts are covered in cobwebby hairs, and its flower heads form fluffy balls. This species is found only in vernal pools, while its smaller sister species, **29-6 *Psilocarphus tenellus* (slender woolly-heads)**, can grow in vernal pools but also on compacted dirt roads.

29-7 *Myosurus minimus* (tiny mousetail) is—astoundingly—a member of the buttercup family. It has simple strap-like leaves and a narrow spike of many tiny flowers. The plants can be numerous and very small or fewer and much larger, a feature common in vernal pool species.

The common blue-flowered **29-8 *Navarretia squarrosa* (skunkweed)** is a member of the phlox family (*Polemoniaceae*). Its leaves are spine-tipped, and it has glands on the tips of its many hairs. As its common name suggests, 29-8 *Navarretia squarrosa* has a skunky odour. A rare smaller, white-flowered species, **29-9 *Navarretia intertexta* (needle-leaved navarretia)**, also grows in vernal pools.

29-10 *Hemizonella minima* (small-headed tarweed) is an uncommon occurrence in rocky, vernally moist spots in the upper-elevation pocket grasslands.

29-11 *Zeltnera muehlenbergii* (Muhlenberg's centaury) is another extremely rare species partial to vernal pool situations. It is a small pink-flowered plant in the gentian family (*Gentianaceae*).

29-12 *Triphysaria versicolor* (bearded owl-clover) occupies the marginal areas around vernal pools. It is part of the owl-clover family (*Orobanchaceae*).

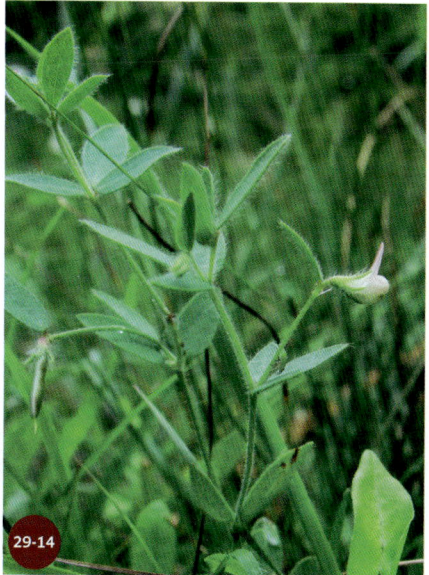

29-13 *Castilleja victoriae* (Victoria's paintbrush) is an extremely rare endemic found in vernal pool habitats on a single offshore islet near Victoria and on Washington state's San Juan Island.

29-14 *Acmispon americanus* (Spanish clover) can also be found on the edges of vernal pools.

Cliff and Talus Habitats

30-1 *Lomatium papilioniferum* **(butterfly bearing lomatium)** is a rare plant restricted to the Gulf Islands. At 35 centimetres and taller, it is one of the larger species in the parsley family. Butterfly bearing lomatium can be very heavily grazed by deer, but its cliffside location is an effective protection against this.

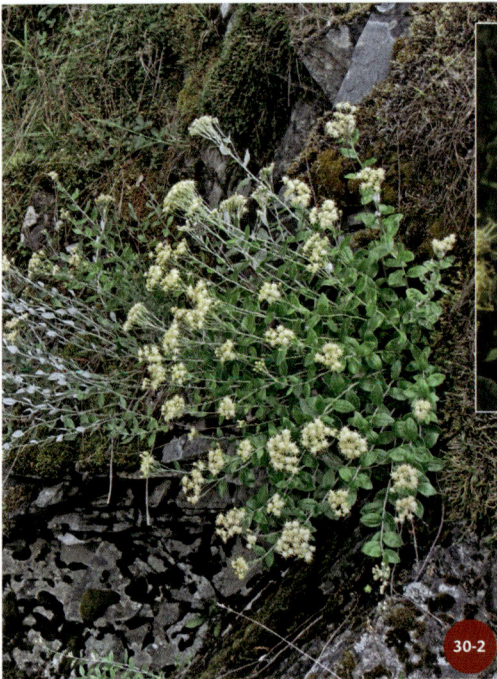

30-2 *Luina hypoleuca* **(silverback luina)** is also found in exposed locations on cliffs. *Luina* is a member of the aster family.

There are also plants that utilize the broken rock below the cliffs. **30-3 *Lomatium dissectum* (fern-leaved desert-parsley)** is one such species. The umbels of its chocolate-brown flowers are held on tall stems up to a metre high. This gives rise to another, more evocative common name for *L. dissectum*: chocolate tips.

One of our most dainty and fragile flowers is **30-4 *Tonella tenella* (small-flowered tonella)**, another plant that usually grows on talus habitats where shaded. The blue flowers, held on hair-thin stems, are similar to those of blue-eyed Mary but only 2 to 4 millimetres across. (A blue-eyed Mary flower is shown near the left centre edge of the image.)

31 Edge and Fringe Habitats

31-1

It may seem odd that such a showy and high-profile plant as **31-1 *Aquilegia formosa* (Sitka columbine)** would not have been covered in earlier sections. However, this beauty is not a classic dry belt species, as it occurs widely in wetter environments and finds its best development in subalpine meadows. Locally, it is restricted to the fringes of forests, especially where they border water courses.

31-2

Another native plant hard to find in any major plant community, but far from being rare, is **31-2 *Geum macrophyllum* (large-leaved avens)**. It typically grows along paths or the edges of fairly moist habitats. Due to the morphology of its whiskery hooked seeds (inset), it distributes itself by catching on the fur of animals or on human clothing.

31-3

Heracleum maximum **(cow parsnip)** is another plant of fringe habitats. Locally, it is found mostly along roadsides or along forest edges where the treed area faces open, often human-created, fields. Its natural distribution is much like the one described for Sitka columbine.

31-4 *Comandra umbellata* ssp. *californica* (California comandra) has also been placed in this edge category perhaps as a result of the few observations for this plant. California comandra barely enters our dry belt from its main distribution further south.

We have dealt with several common species that colonize slides and seepy banks, such as 4-8 *Equisetum telmateia* (giant horsetail), 5-12 *Equisetum hyemale* (scouring rush) and 3-6 *Tellima grandiflora* (fringecup). An uncommon new species under such conditions, usually found under deciduous trees, is **32-1 *Angelica genuflexa* (kneeling angelica)**. The specific name *genuflexa* translates as "with bended knees," referring to the odd downward bend in the stalks that attach the leaves to the stem, visible in the central section of our image and highlighted in the inset. This is one of two species of this genus that occur in the coastal dry belt. The other, *Angelica lucida* (seacoast angelica, not pictured), is an uncommon inhabitant of estuary meadows.

Fresh slides in often treeless sections of this habitat harbour **32-2 *Petasites frigidus* var. *palmatus* (sweet coltsfoot)**. Coltsfoot consistently colonizes moving-earth habitats.

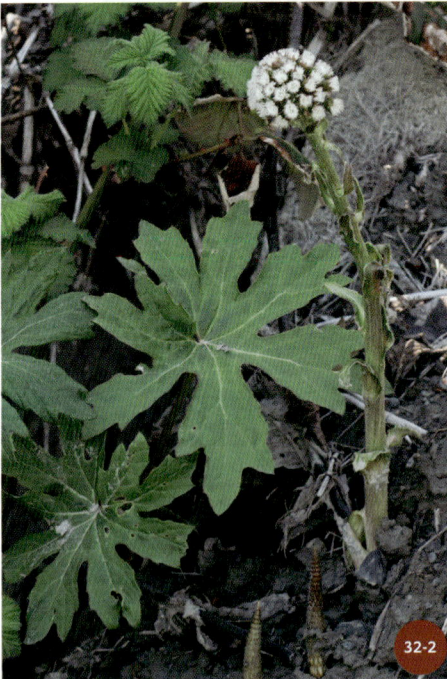

33 *Castilleja* "Habitats"?

Finally, to conclude this guide, let us consider the paintbrushes. We have three perennial species, one of them quite rare. Of course, there is no definable habitat for any of them (hence the question mark), as they are parasites, and their growing sites are determined by their host plants. Nevertheless, we can try to indicate where they are *usually* found.

    Castilleja hispida and *Castilleja miniata* var. *miniata* (not pictured but a close relative of var. *dixonii*) are most abundant and spectacular in alpine meadows.

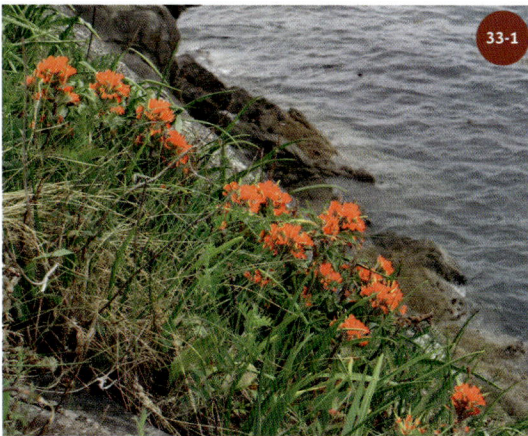

33-1 *Castilleja hispida* (harsh paintbrush) is the least predictable. It may be found on steep banks facing the ocean or in higher-elevation woodlands or grasslands.

33-2 *Castilleja miniata* var. *dixonii* (Dixon's scarlet paintbrush) tends to grow on earthy and rocky slopes and cliffs facing the ocean, primarily in the Gulf Islands region.

We end with **33-3 *Castilleja levisecta* (golden paintbrush)**. This rare and endangered species is restricted to small offshore islands.

"Those who contemplate the beauty of the earth find reserves of strength that will endure as long as life lasts."

Rachel Carson, 1907–1964

Appendix: Foreign Species Invasions

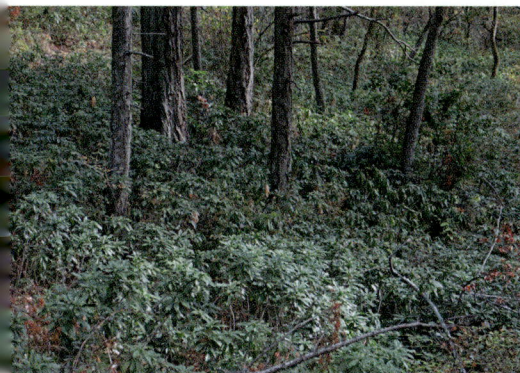

Daphne laureola (spurge daphne) invasion in a dry Douglas-fir forest.

Ilex aquifolium (English holly) occupying this forest's tall shrub and lower tree layer.

Crataegus monogyna (common hawthorn) occupying what used to be Garry oak parkland.

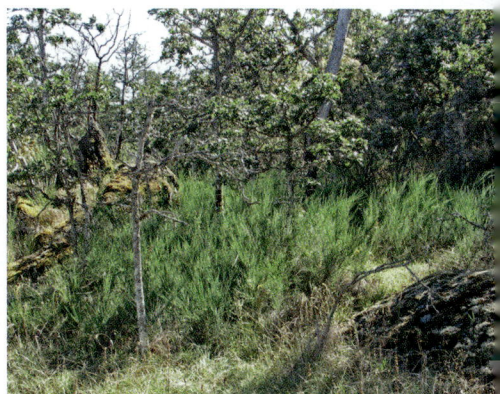

Cytisus scoparius (Scotch broom) invasion in a Garry oak woodland.

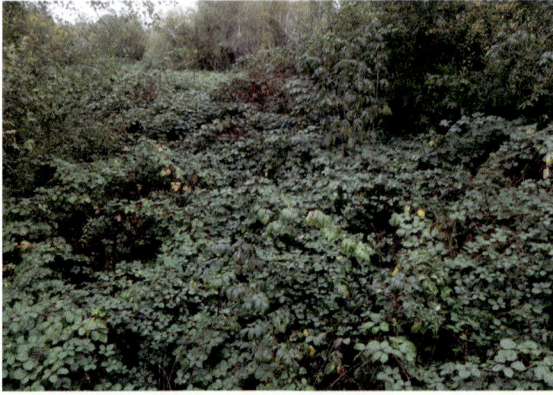

Rubus armeniacus (Himalayan blackberry) smothers everything in some moist habitats.

Hedera helix (English ivy) is a common invader in many dry belt forest types.

Phalaris arundinacea (reed canarygrass) is the bane of all local wetlands. The thatch of this grass can become so dense as to choke out all herbaceous wetland vegetation. It is capable of forming floating mats that can go up and down with water levels.

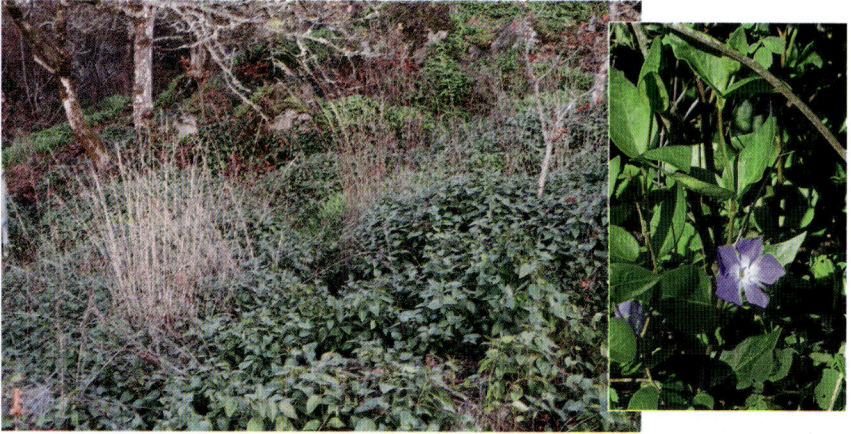

Vinca major (large periwinkle) is a serious invader in suburban Garry oak ecosystems. Spreading from underground rhizomes, it is difficult to remove once established.

Garden Escapes

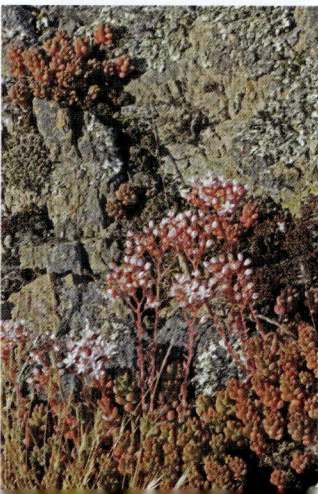

Several of the foreign plants that have invaded native plant communities in the coastal dry belt originated in flower gardens. Examples shown here are *Oxalis* sp. (a garden hybrid of wood sorrel) in forests, *Lamium galeobdolon* (yellow archangel) in woodlands, *Hyacinthoides × massartiana* (hybrid bluebells) in Garry oak meadows and Sedum album (white stonecrop) on rocky habitats.

Common garden escapees also include (top left) *Muscari armeniacum* (Armenian grape hyacinth) in dry Garry oak openings, (top right) *Cyclamen hederifolium* (cyclamen) in woodlands and forests, and (above) *Doronicum pardalianches* (great leopard's-bane) in forests.

Foreign Weedy Grasses

Non-native grasses are both indicators for, and agents of, ecosystem degradation in open habitats of the Garry oak ecosystem. They come in two forms, as annuals and as perennials. Some examples of the worst offenders are shown.

Annuals

These grasses grow from seed each year and are capable of colonizing both shallow and deep soils.

Bromus hordeaceus (soft brome); *Bromus diandrus* ssp. *rigidus* (rip-gut brome); *Bromus sterilis* (barren brome); *Cynosurus echinatus* (hedgehog dogtail).

Top to bottom: *Vulpia bromoides* (barren fescue); *Aira praecox* (early hairgrass); mix of *Bromus* species. The pink flowers and green leaves are *Convolvulus arvensis* (field bindweed), another European introduction.

Perennials

These grasses have overwintering basal leaf clusters from which they can grow new shoots every year. They require deeper soils or rock crevices to survive.

Anthoxanthum odoratum (sweet vernalgrass) growing on a steep slope, apparently rooted in a deep crevice.

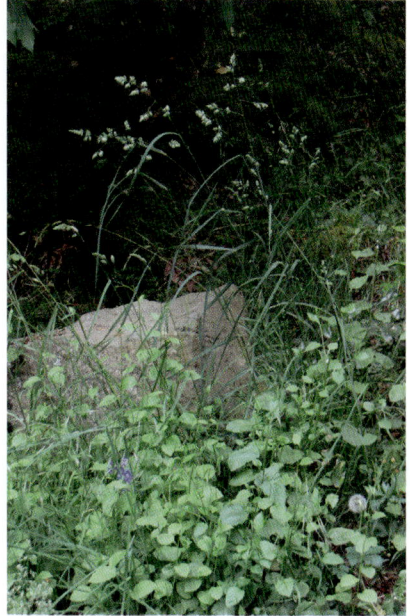

Dactylis glomerata (orchard grass), a large grass, is shown here in association with another invader, *Alliaria petiolata* (garlic mustard).

Holcus lanatus (common velvet-grass) with closed and open panicles.

Poa pratensis (Kentucky bluegrass) inflorescences at maturity. Inset shows rhizomes of the species.

Unfortunately, as many of us have long suspected, perhaps the most invasive species remains *Homo sapiens*. Here is an example where an ignorant or irresponsible person on a motorcycle ploughed through this pristine meadow of satinflowers (*Olsynium douglasii*) before the flowers burst into bloom. The track created will no doubt form an avenue for further invasion of non-native grasses and other weeds, not to speak of the potential for water erosion along this groove of seepage-saturated terrain.

Bibliography, References & Information Sources

Acker, Maleea. *Gardens Aflame: Garry Oak Meadows of BC's South Coast*. Vancouver, BC: New Star Books, 2012.

Barkworth, M.E., K.M. Capels, S. Long, L.K. Anderton, M.B. Piep, eds. *Manual of Grasses for North America*. Logan, UT: Utah State University Press, 2007.

Bowcutt, F., and S. Hamman, eds. *Vascular Plants of the South Sound Prairies*. Olympia, WA: Evergreen State College Press, 2016.

Bowcutt, Frederica. "Creation of a Field Guide to Camas Prairie Plants with Undergraduates: Project-Based Learning Combined with Epistemological Decolonization." *Ethnobiology Letters*, 12(1):21-31, 2021.

Brayshaw, T.C. "Catkin Bearing Plants of British Columbia." Occasional Paper No. 18. Victoria, BC: Royal British Columbia Museum, 1976.

Brayshaw, T.C. "Buttercups, Waterlilies and Their Relatives in British Columbia." Victoria, BC: Royal British Columbia Museum, Memoir No. 1, 1989.

British Columbia Conservation Data Centre, Province of British Columbia. Species and Ecosystem Explorer, 2017. http://a100.gov.bc.ca/pub/eswp/ [last accessed June 2024].
Authors' note: This site was probably the most frequently used in the creation of this guide. As mentioned in the text, all plant names in the guide are based on those referenced on this site, as are comments on rarity. For BC's vascular plants, the contents of the Species and Ecosystem Explorer are updated every year by the BC Flora Committee, a group of botanical experts that includes this book's senior author.

Brodie, H.J. "The Splash-cup Dispersal Mechanism in Plants." *Canadian Journal of Botany*, 29 (3):224-234, 1951.

Brodo, I.M., Sylvia D. Sharnoff, and Stephen Sharnoff. *Lichens of North America*. New Haven, CT: Yale University Press, 2001.

Camp, Pamela, and John G. Gamon, eds. *Field Guide to the Rare Plants of Washington*. Seattle, WA: University of Washington Press, 2011.

Clark, L.J. *Wildflowers of British Columbia*. Sidney, BC: Gray's Publishing Ltd., 1973.

Conard, Henry, and Paul Redfearn. *How to Know the Mosses and Liverworts*, second edition. Dubuque, IA: William C. Brown Company Publishers, 1979.

Consortium of Pacific Northwest Herbaria. http://www.pnwherbaria.org/ [last accessed June 2024].
Authors' note: A portal to over 3.6 million specimen records of the Pacific Northwest's 60 herbaria. Areas represented include Alaska, British Columbia, Idaho, Montana, Oregon, Washington & Yukon Territory. Upon entering a valid scientific plant name, this site brings up a map of the Pacific

Northwest where each collection of the plant is registered by herbarium with collections attributes and shown as a circle after the map is enlarged to a suitable scale. The site was primarily used to ascertain the geographical distribution of plant species. Where identification of certain taxa presents difficulties, the site is also useful to compare morphological features on photographs of herbarium sheets, if they are provided.

Darris, D., S. Johnson, and A. Bartow. "Plant Fact Sheet for Roemer's Fescue (*Festuca roemeri*)." Corvallis, OR: USDA Natural Resources Conservation Service, Plant Materials Center, May 2006, revised July 2012.

Deur, Douglas, and Nancy J. Turner, eds. *Keeping It Living: Traditions of Plant Use and Cultivation on the Northwest Coast of North America*. Vancouver, BC: University of British Columbia Press, and Seattle, WA: University of Washington Press, 2005.

Douglas, G.W. "The Sunflower Family (*Asteraceae*) of British Columbia. Volume I – Senecioneae." Occasional Paper No. 23. Victoria, BC: Royal British Columbia Museum, 1982.

Douglas, G.W., G.B. Straley, and D. Meidinger. "The Vascular Plants of British Columbia Part 1: Gymnosperms and Dicotyledons (*Aceraceae* through *Cucurbitaceae*)." Special Report, Series 1. Victoria, BC: British Columbia Ministry of Forests, Research Branch, 1989.

Douglas, G.W., G.B. Straley, and D. Meidinger. "The Vascular Plants of British Columbia Part 2: Dicotyledons (*Diapensiaceae* through *Portulacaceae*)." Special Report, Series 2. Victoria, BC: British Columbia Ministry of Forests, Research Branch, 1990.

Douglas, G.W., G.B. Straley, and D. Meidinger. "The Vascular Plants of British Columbia Part 3: Dicotyledons (*Primulaceae* through *Zygophyllaceae*)." Special Report, Series 3. Victoria, BC: British Columbia Ministry of Forests, Research Branch, 1991.

Douglas, G.W., G.B. Straley, and D. Meidinger. "The Vascular Plants of British Columbia Part 4: Monocotyledons." Special Report, Series 4. Victoria, BC: British Columbia Ministry of Forests, Research Branch, 1994.

Douglas, J. "Report to McLoughlin, July 12, 1842." Cited in "Founding of Victoria," *The Beaver*, Outfit 273, March 1943.

Dunwiddie, P.W., and E.R Alverson. "Prairies, Savannas, and Oak Woodlands of the Pacific Northwest." *Reference Module in Earth Systems and Environmental Sciences*. Elsevier, ScienceDirect, 2019.

E-Flora BC: Electronic Atlas of the Plants of British Columbia. http://www.eflora.bc.ca/ [last accessed June 2024].

Authors' note: E-Flora BC is an online biogeographic atlas of the flora (vascular plants, bryophytes, lichens and algae), fungi and slime moulds of British Columbia. The majority of BC's vascular plant flora is presented in photographs on this site, usually in multiple images for each species. A useful resource not only for viewing comparative images but also for accessing alternate vernacular names.

Erickson, W.R. *Classification and Interpretation of Garry Oak* (Quercus garryana) *Plant Communities and Ecosystems in Southwestern British Columbia*. MSc thesis. Victoria, BC: University of Victoria Department of Geography, 1996.

Flora of North America Editorial Committee, eds. *Flora of North America North of Mexico*, 30 vols. New York, NY, and Oxford, UK: Oxford University Press, 1993. http://floranorthamerica.org [last accessed June 2024].

Authors' note: This work is only partially completed, at present to volume 16, and is being updated continuously. It will eventually be the authoritative flora for North America.

Grant, W.C. "Report on Vancouver Island." Manuscript. Victoria, BC: Provincial Archives of British Columbia, 1849.

Green, R.N., and K. Klinka. "A Field Guide for Site Identification and Interpretation for the Vancouver Forest Region." *Land Management Handbook*. BC Ministry of Forests, Research Branch, 1994. https://www.for.gov.bc.ca/hfd/pubs/docs/lmh/lmh28.htm [last accessed June 2024].

Hamman, S.T., P.W. Dunwiddie, J.L. Nuckols, and M. McKinley. "Fire as a Restoration Tool in Pacific Northwest Prairies and Oak Woodlands: Challenges, Successes, and Future Directions." *Northwest Science*, 85:317, 2011.

Hitchcock, C.L., and A. Cronquist. *Flora of the Pacific Northwest: An Illustrated Manual*, second edition. Seattle, WA: University of Washington Press, 2018.

Hughes B. *History of the Comox Valley*. Nanaimo, BC: Evergreen Press, 1962.

Jennings, Neil L. *Popular Wildflowers of Coastal British Columbia and Vancouver Island*. Surrey, BC: Rocky Mountain Books, 2020.

Klinka, K., F.C. Nuszdorfer, and L. Skoda. "Biogeoclimatic Units of Central and Southern Vancouver Island." Province of British Columbia, Ministry of Forests, 1979.

Kozloff, E.N. *Plants of Western Oregon, Washington and British Columbia*. Portland, OR: Timber Press, 2005.

Lawton, Elva. "Moss Flora of the Pacific Northwest." Supplement No. 1 of the *Journal of the Hattori Botanical Laboratory*. Nichinan-shi, Miyazaki, Japan, 1971.

MacKinnon, A., and Kem Luther. *Mushrooms of British Columbia*. Victoria, BC: Royal British Columbia Museum, 2021.

McCune B., and Linda Geiser. *Macrolichens of the Pacific Northwest*. Corvallis, OR: Oregon State University Press, 1997. Co-published with the USDA Forest Service.

Meidinger, D., and J. Pojar, eds. "Ecosystems of British Columbia." Special Report, Series No. 6. Victoria, BC: British Columbia Ministry of Forests, Research Branch, 1991. https://www.for.gov.bc.ca/hfd/pubs/Docs/Srs/Srs06.htm [last accessed June 2024].
Authors' note: Meidinger and Pojar (1991) divide the Douglas-fir forest into a "Douglas-fir–Salal" and a "Douglas-fir–Shore Pine–Arbutus" community. As the total species combination of the two are very similar and show broad transitions, it is important to note that in the central and northern part of the dry belt, and on sandy soils on some of the neighbouring islands, shore pine can be an additional tree species. It should also be pointed out that the Douglas-fir, arbutus and shore pine trees in this guide also occur at a higher elevation in combination with pocket grasslands, but that our "Shore Pine–Douglas-fir–Arbutus Woodland" (Section 8) has little overlap otherwise with Meidinger and Pojar's community named above.

Miller, M., and Hans Roemer. Draft COSEWIC Status Report on Fragrant Popcorn Flower, *Plagiobothrys figuratus*. Prepared for the Committee on the Status of Endangered Wildlife in Canada. Submitted January 2005, Victoria, BC.

Nesom, G.L. "Taxonomy of *Erythranthe* sect. *Simiola* (Phrymaceae) in the USA and Mexico." *Phytoneuron* 40: 1-123 (PDF), 2012.

Nesom, G.L. "The Taxonomic Status of *Mimulus sookensis* (Phrymaceae) and Comments on Related Aspects of Biology in Species of *Erythranthe*." *Phytoneuron* 2013-69: 1-18, 2013.

Nuszdorfer, F.C., K. Klinka, and D.A. Demarchi. "Chapter 5: Coastal Douglas-fir Zone." *Ecosystems of British Columbia*. Victoria, BC: BC Ministry of Forests, 1991. Compiled and edited by Del Meidinger and Jim Pojar.

Pojar, J., and A. Mackinnon. *Plants of Coastal British Columbia including Washington, Oregon and Alaska*. Vancouver, BC: Lone Pine Publishing, 1994.

Pojar, J., A. MacKinnon, J. Fenneman, and L. Joseph (Styawat). *Vascular Plants of Coastal British Columbia and the Pacific Northwest*. Forthcoming.

Pojar, J., K. Klinka, and D.V. Meidinger. "Biogeoclimatic Ecosystem Classification in British Columbia." *Forest Ecology and Management*, Vol. 22, Issues 1–2, 1987.

Pojar, Rosamund. *What's in a Name? The Meaning and Derivation of Common and Latin Names of Plants in British Columbia*. Smithers, BC: Cassiope Press, 2021.

Roemer, H.L. *Forest Vegetation and Environments on the Saanich Peninsula, Vancouver Island*. PhD dissertation. Victoria, BC: University of Victoria, 1972.

Roemer, H. "Rare Plant and Plant Species Inventory for Fort Rodd Hill/Fisgard Lighthouse National Historic Sites." Unpublished report prepared for Parks Canada, 2002.

Roemer, H. "Plant Species at Risk on Little Saanich Mountain." Unpublished survey carried out for the National Research Council of Canada, 2003.

Roemer, H. "The Puzzle of the Rare Prairie Lupine." *Menziesia* Vol. 10, Issue 3, 2005.

Roemer, H. Draft COSEWIC Status Report on Gray's Desert Parsley, *Lomatium grayi* (Coult. & Rose). Prepared for the Committee on the Status of Endangered Wildlife in Canada. Submitted January 2005.

Roemer, H. Annual reports, 2007–2010 and 2012–2015, each titled "Rare Plant Monitoring, Mill Hill Regional Park."

Roemer, H. "Critical Habitat Survey for Prairie Lupine." Unpublished report and mapping prepared for the Garry Oak Ecosystems Recovery Team, Victoria, BC, September 2009.

Roemer, H. "Introduced Plants: Just How Exotic Are We?" Garry Oak Ecosystems Recovery Team, Research Colloquium, 2009.

Roemer, H. "Impact of Grazing and Competing Vegetation on a Population of the Endangered Yellow Montane Violet on Mt. Tuam." Year 4 report prepared for Transport Canada, NAV Canada, Garry Oak Ecosystem Recovery Team, Conservation Data Centre, and Canadian Wildlife Service, 2010.

Roemer, H. "Rare Plant Monitoring, Mill Hill Regional Park." Summary Report, 2015.

Roemer, H. "Rare Vascular Plants, Lichens and Ecological Communities on Mt. Finlayson." Unpublished study prepared for WSP Environmental Services, 2019.

Roemer, H., and Carrina Maslovat. "Species Stewardship Account for White Meconella (*Meconella oregana*)." Unpublished report prepared for the Garry Oak Ecosystems Recovery Team, Victoria, BC, 2004.

Roemer, H., and Matt Fairbarns. "Red and Blue Listed Plants of the Somenos Garry Oak Protected Area." Unpublished survey undertaken for the Garry Oak Ecosystems Recovery Team, Victoria, BC, 2003.

Roemer, H., and R. Batten. "Vegetation Inventory and Mapping in the Chemainus River Estuary." Unpublished report prepared for Ducks Unlimited Canada, September 2014.

Roemer, H., Adolf Ceska, and Oldriska Ceska. "Conservation Values of an Eagle Heights Protected Area." Unpublished report prepared for Regional Director, Vancouver Island Region, BC Ministry of Water, Land and Air Protection, Nanaimo, BC, February 2003.

Savile, D.B. "Splash-cup Dispersal Mechanism in *Chrysosplenium* and *Mitella*." *Science*, Vol. 117, 1953.

Stearn, W.T. *Stearn's Dictionary of Plant Names for Gardeners*. Portland, OR: Timber Press, 2002.

Taylor, T.M.C. *Pacific Northwest Ferns and Their Allies*. Toronto, ON: University of Toronto Press, 1970.

Taylor, T.M.C. *The Sedge Family of British Columbia*, Handbook 43. Victoria, BC: British Columbia Provincial Museum, 1983.

Tropicos.org.

> *Authors' note: This database links over 1.37M scientific names with over 6.74M specimens and over 1.31M digital images. This site is one of several botanical databases where correct names and their botanical underpinnings can be looked up (compare entry under VASCAN).*

Turner, Mark, and Phyllis Gustafson. *Wildflowers of the Pacific Northwest*. Portland, OR: Timber Press, 2006.

Turner, N.J., and H.V. Kuhnlein. "Two Important 'Root' Foods of the Northwest Coast Indians: Springbank clover (*Trifolium wormskioldii*) and Pacific silverweed (*Potentilla anserina* ssp. *pacifica*)." *Economic Botany* 36(4):411-432, 1982.

Turner, Nancy J. *Food Plants of Coastal First Peoples*. Victoria, BC: Royal British Columbia Museum Handbooks, 2006.

University of Washington Herbarium. See Consortium of Pacific Northwest Herbaria. https://www.pnwherbaria.org/data/search.php [last accessed June 2024].

VASCAN, the Database of Vascular Plants of Canada.

> *Authors' note: VASCAN is a comprehensive list of the vascular plants of Canada, Greenland (Denmark) and Saint Pierre and Miquelon (France). For each species, sub-species and variety, VASCAN provides the accepted scientific name (in Latin), accepted vernacular name in French and English, synonyms or alternative names, plant distribution status (native, introduced, etc.) and habit of the plant (tree, shrub, herb or vine). VASCAN also includes a distribution map by province or territory and can generate lists of taxa according to various criteria (distribution, habit, etc.). VASCAN data can be downloaded. https://data.canadensys.net/vascan/search [last accessed June 2024]. See also entry under Tropicos, a site for worldwide searches and with more features offered. However, VASCAN is probably the more pertinent tool for our area due to its narrower range.*

Photo Credits

- Rick Avis: *Artemisia campestris* ssp. *pacifica*, p. 158, image 15-10 and inset photo.
- Ryan Batten: *Lomatium papilioniferum*, p. 226, image 30-1 and *Eleocharis parvula*, p. 180, image 18-19 (inset).
- Curtis Bjork: *Atriplex gmelinii*, p. 161, image 15-16 (2 images).
- Jamie Fenneman: *Angelica genuflexa*, p. 230, image 32-1 (inset).
- Judith Holm: *Spergularia canadensis*, p. 152, image 14-6.
- Kristen Miskelly: *Hydrophyllum tenuipes*, p. 67, image 6-11.
- Lisa Spellacy: The authors at Harling Point, Oak Bay, p. 264.
- Ken Wong: *Nuttallanthus texanus*, p. 202, image 22-6.
- All other images provided by the authors.

Glossary of Botanical and Ecological Terms

annual: Annuals are plants that complete their entire life cycle (from seed to new seed) in a single year (compare *perennial*).

axillary: Located in or arising from a leaf axil.

bract: A simplified leaf blade that subtends a flower/fruit or the entire cluster of flowers/fruits.

bryophyte: A general term including mosses and liverworts.

carnivorous: Plants that prey on and can digest insects.

corm: A thickened underground stem that serves as a storage organ.

corolla: The totality of all petals in a flower.

cotyledon: The first leaf that develops upon germination of a seed. Monocotyledons such as lilies or grasses ("monocots") develop a germination leaf consisting of a single blade (compare *dicots*).

cover estimates (cover values): The area (%) covered by a particular species within a vegetation sample plot.

culm: The above-ground stem of a grass or sedge.

deciduous: Trees or shrubs that lose their leaves in winter (deciduous vs. evergreen trees).

dicots: Abbreviated form of dicotyledons, plants that develop following a germination leaf with two blades (compare *monocots*).

emergent: Plants rooted in the ground under water but reaching or exceeding the water surface with foliage and flowering parts.

forbs: Herbaceous flowering plants other than grasses, sedges and rushes.

geophytes: Plants with underground storage systems: e.g., thickened roots, tubers, corms and bulbs.

glaucous: With a greyish or blueish surface.

glume(s): The lowest two bracts of a spikelet in grasses, usually different in size (first glume, second glume).

herbaceous: That portion of vegetation that consists of non-woody green plants.

inflorescence: The cluster or arrangement of flowers, usually at the end of a flowering shoot.

involucre: A set of bracts that envelope or wrap around a plant's inflorescence.

lemma: The next bract upward from the glumes in a grass spikelet, bearing the male or female organs. Grasses with a spike-like configuration may have many lemmas.

ligulate flowering parts: Flowering heads in the aster family contain two kinds of flowers, those with flattened blades (female) and those with a tubular structure (male). Those with flattened blades are referred to as a "ligulate."

ligule: A small appendage on the upper side of the leaf base in grasses, usually wrapped around the culm.

monocots: Abbreviated form of monocotyledons, plants that develop following a single germination leaf (compare *dicots*).

panicle: A many-branched inflorescence common in grasses.

pappus: A modified calyx in the aster family, sometimes divided into threads and prominent hairs that help in the wind dispersal of seeds, often by forming parachute-like structures.

pedicel: The stalk of a single flower in an inflorescence.

peduncle: The stalk of a flower or of an inflorescence.

perennial: A plant that can flower and survive several years without growing from a new seed (compare *annual*).

perianth: The sepals and petals (or tepals) of a flower, collectively.

perigynium: A special bract that encloses the seed of *Carex*, usually sack- or bottle-shaped.

petals: In most flowers, the petals are the inner ring of coloured members, surrounded by an outer ring of sepals, which are usually green.

petiole: The stalk of a leaf (compare *peduncle*).

pinnae (plural): Used in describing the structure of a fern. Ferns have pinnae (the first order of leafy side branches) on which pinnules (the second order) are attached.

pinnules: The leafy side branchlets attached to the pinnae in ferns.

pistillate: Flowers that have pistils, the female, but not the male, flowering parts.

pubescent: Bearing hairs of any kind.

relevé: A complete list of plant species that occur on an area of pre-defined size, intended to be a sample for a specific type of vegetation (each species usually listed with a cover/abundance value).

rhizomatous: Bearing rhizomes.

rhizome: A creeping underground stem.

sepals: The outer ring of (usually green) members of a flower, subtending the coloured petals.

spike: Flowers or seeds arranged along an axis.

spikelet: The individual flowering portion in grasses. Spikelets may be arranged in a panicle, or they can form a spike if attached to the main axis of the culm.

stamen: The male part in a flower.

staminate: Flowers that have stamens, the male, but not the female, flowering parts.

stigma: A component of the female part in a flower that receives pollen from pollinators.

successional stage: The stage of development of a plant community. A term usually used for plant communities in an early or a later stage of development. Species combinations can change from one to another successional stage.

tepal: A sepal or petal, or member of an undifferentiated perianth.

tuber: The thickened part of a rhizome utilized as a storage organ.

vernal pool: A shallow depression that remains wet or water-filled when surrounding habitats have already dried off.

zygomorphic: Bilaterally symmetrical but not radially symmetrical.

Index

Numbers in boldface indicate pages with a photo of the plant

Arbutus menziesii (arbutus).

About the Authors

Hans Roemer is an ecologist with extensive experience in studying plant communities and ecosystems. His academic credentials and decades of fieldwork in British Columbia have made him a respected authority on the native plants of the region.

Mary Sanseverino is a photographer and former computer science faculty member at the University of Victoria. Her expertise in photography and passion for the natural world complement her co-authorship, bringing the beauty of BC's native plants to life.

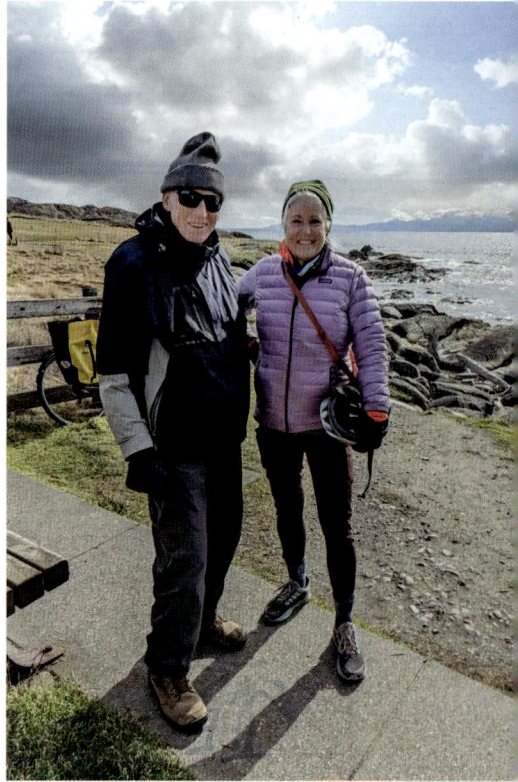